C000128019

Daily Joy

Anne Holton is a Sister of Mercy at St Leo's Convent of Mercy, Carlow, and works as a Diocesan Advisor in religious education. She holds a doctorate in theology and religious education and lectures at Carlow College, St Patrick's, Carlow. She is also the author of *Liberating Spirituality for Religious Educators* (Wyndham Hall Press, 2002).

Daily Joy

A Collection of Well-loved Spiritual Writings

Edited by Anne Holton

Dedicated to my family in Clonaugh, Moyvalley, Co. Kildare; my community, St Leo's Convent of Mercy, Carlow; teachers of Kildare and Leighlin; students of Carlow College, St Patrick's, Carlow; and my many friends.

Living Wide Open: Landscapes of the Mind

I will not die an unlived life
I will not live in fear
of falling or catching fire.
I choose to inhabit my days,
to allow my living to open me,
to make me less afraid,
more accessible;
to loosen my heart
until it becomes a wing,
a torch, a promise.
I choose to risk my significance
To live so that which came to me as a seed
goes to the next as blossom,
and that which came to me as blossom,
goes on in fruit …

Dawna Markova

Published 2011 by
Veritas Publications
7–8 Lower Abbey Street
Dublin 1
Ireland
publications@veritas.ie
www.veritas.ie

ISBN 978-1-84730-322-6

10 9 8 7 6 5 4 3 2

A catalogue record for this book is available from the British Library.

Designed by Dara O'Connor, Veritas
Printed in Ireland by Gemini International, Dublin

Veritas books are printed on paper made from the wood pulp of managed forests. For every tree felled, at least one tree is planted, thereby renewing natural resources.

Contents

A Better Self

Lessons from Nature

Knowing and Celebrating God

Advent and Christmas

Introduction

I have gathered together in this book a collection of spiritual writings – some of which I used at the beginning of lectures in Carlow College, St Patrick's, where I gave a copy to each student on which to reflect. The students expressed their appreciation and so I decided to put a selection into book form, so that it might enrich the lives of others. I have been privileged to deal with teachers of the present and the future and have learned much from them. Sincere thanks. It has been a privilege for me to be an instrument in liberating people into the glorious freedom of being children of God.

The secularism of our time cannot be met by argument. It is never a matter of imposing Christ, but recommending him as supremely attractive to all people. We try to educate the whole person – head, heart and hand. Unlike the dualistic, divisive impact of doctrines about how bad and unworthy we are, we need the reassurance that we are already shining with the presence of a God who is utterly at home with us. This is positively transforming for human beings. This is what happened in Jesus Christ. In him it was revealed that God's heart beats in all our hearts, that our bodies are temples of the Holy Spirit, and that every creature is a divine work of art.

It is often said that we are not human beings trying to be spiritual, we are spiritual beings trying to become more human. The graced unfolding of our lives is God's dream within us becoming true. It is about being truly human, each in their own unique way, and thus interpreting God's love story in the language of our modern age and so helping people to read that same story in the wonder of their own being – even in the ambiguity of their lives. The whole point of Christ's coming was to bring an abundance to people's lives by his very presence. It is God's delight to be dwelling within us.

Our task is to convince ourselves and all people that we are unconditionally loved by God, who is so delighted to be intimately one with us. The first concern of Jesus was to set people free from their despair to live a more abundant life here and now and to bring joy into their daily lives. This is our task now. May the reflections in this book help us to let this become a reality in our lives, and so receive it and live the good news of Scripture: 'I came that you may have life and have it to the full' (Jn 10:10).

This book is for everyone. Just pick it up and read one reflection at a time. It will help focus you to the great reality that Jesus is present to us always, as he promised, especially in our most ordinary actions. This is what the Incarnation we celebrate at Christmas means: God has become human and nothing human is alien to God – so please don't keep him at a distance, or just for special places and prayers. Yes, God is present there too – and these are important places and actions to focus us – but we ought to wake up to the fact that he pervades all our lives, with its ups and downs. He will see us through all our journeys. Sometimes we glimpse him in the beauty of creation and other times in the darkness of pain and loss, and all works together for good if we persevere. These few reflections may help to focus us, as it is easy to forget that the invisible God is with us in all.

God bless you.

Sr Anne Holton

Teaching and Learning

Between Teacher and Child

I have come to a frightening conclusion. I am the decisive element in the classroom. It is my personal approach that creates the climate. It is my daily mood that makes the weather. As a teacher, I possess tremendous power to make a child's life miserable or joyous. I can humiliate or humour, hurt or heal. In all situations it is my response that decides whether a crisis may be escalated or de-escalated, and a child humanised or de-humanised.

Dr Haim G. Ginott

Blessing for a Teacher

You are blessed

You hold the children,
the gift of creation,
in the palm of your hand

You hold the spirits of God
close to your heart

You form the minds
You inspire the hearts
You shape the hopes
of the children
of the future
of the Kingdom of God

You bless the children
with the gift of yourself

They bless you in return
with promise fulfilled
with hope realised
with life well done

Margaret Cessna HM

God Created Teachers

On the sixth day, God created men and women.

On the seventh day, he rested.

No so much to recuperate, but rather to prepare himself for the work he was going to do the next day. For it was on that day – the eighth day – that God created the first teacher.

This teacher, though taken from among men and women, had several significant modifications. In general, God made the teacher more durable than other men and women. The teacher was made to arise at a very early hour and go to bed no earlier than 11.30 p.m. with no rest in between.

The teacher had to be able to withstand being locked up in an airtight classroom for six hours with thirty-five 'monsters' on a rainy Monday. And the teacher had to be fit to correct 103 exam papers over Easter holidays.

Yes, God made the teacher tough … but gentle too. The teacher was equipped with soft hands to wipe away the tears of the neglected and lonely student … those of the sixteen-year-old girl who was not asked to the dance.

And into the teacher God poured a generous amount of patience. Patience when a student asks the teacher to repeat the directions they've just repeated for someone else. Patience when the kids forget their lunch money for the fourth day in a row. Patience when one-third of the class fails the test. Patience when the textbooks haven't arrived yet and the semester starts tomorrow.

And God gave the teacher a heart slightly bigger than the average human heart. For the teacher's heart had to be big enough to love the kid who screams, 'I hate this class – it's boring!' and to love the kid who runs out of the classroom at the end of the period without so much as a 'goodbye', let alone a 'thank you'.

And lastly, God gave the teacher an abundant supply of hope. For God knew that the teacher would always be hoping. Hoping that the kids would someday learn how to spell … Hoping not to have lunchroom duty … Hoping that Friday would come … Hoping for a free day … Hoping for deliverance.

When God finished creating the teacher, he stepped back and admired the work at his hands. And God saw that the teacher was good. Very good!

And God smiled, for when he looked at the teacher, he saw into the future. He knew that the future is in the hands of the teachers.

And because God loves teachers so much, on the ninth day God created 'snow days'.

Author unknown

Christ's Way of Teaching

The foundation on which everything was built was his relationship with people.
People felt he was right there with them.
He talked their language.
He used their experiences to make his point.
He put himself in their position.
He made them feel that they were important.
He was open to them – all of the time.
He respected people deeply and loved them greatly.
He would never force himself upon them, even to make them do what was best for them. Rather, he allowed and enabled them to see for themselves.

He used the experience of the moment.
A sudden quarrel among the disciples.
A man let down through the roof.
A sneer from the Pharisees.
A news item about a nasty incident at the temple.
All these and many other incidents became the basis of his teaching.

He always adapted his teaching to those he taught.
He started with people just where they were.
He didn't ask them to be cleverer, or to believe this or that, before he could teach them.

He didn't just tell people what he wanted them to know, he made them work it out for themselves.
How often he refused to give a direct answer to a question!
He didn't have readymade answers.
Rather, by his words, he stimulated people into conversation until they suddenly saw the thing for themselves.

He made use of visual aids.
A child, a farmer, flowers in the fields, mustard seeds, a sunset.

Finally, and probably most important, he taught his close disciples very often by plunging them into a great experience, in which they had to put into practice everything they had learned so far.
For example, the mission of the twelve, and later the seventy-two. In another sense, their living with him day by day was the most effective education of all.

Author unknown

Paraphrase of St Paul's Letter to the Corinthians

I Corinthians 13:1-8

Though I teach in ways that are pleasing to the administrators
but do not have love toward the children,
I am no better than a foghorn or a loud speaker.

And though I am proficient in the science of pedagogy,
and hold certificates in all advanced degrees
but do not love my pupils, all of my degrees are worthless.

And even though I have studied child psychology
and know all about the id and about environmental conditions,
yet if I do not actively love my children, it profits very little.

And though I know the subject inside and out,
and have a very good blackboard manner,
if I have not love in my heart, I achieve precisely nothing.

Love makes a teacher have infinite patience –
Love searches out every avenue, during class or in my own time
to be helpful to a backward child.

Love does not try to manipulate children –
does not talk down to them, nor try to turn them into fan clubs
who will idolise their teacher.

Love does not insist that every child progress
at a uniform speed, pleasing the teacher,
and makes allowances for individual endowments and differences.

Love has good manners,
and respects a child as a whole person
in the sight of God and of men.

Love is not touchy or temperamental,
and does not take out the frustrations of home
on the children in class.

Love teaches children to be forgiving
by showing that we as teachers
do not hold grudges against them.

Love does not point out
or ridicule the slow learners,
but rejoices exceedingly when they make progress.

Love knows no limit to its patience,
no end to its hope,
no fading of its encouragement.

It is, in fact,
the one quality that denotes a real teacher –
and a real person.

Author unknown

All I Really Need to Know I Learned in Kindergarten

All I really needed to know about how to live and what to do and how to be, I learned in kindergarten. Wisdom was not at the top of the graduate-school mountain, but there in the sand pile at Sunday school. These are the things I learned:

Share everything.

Play fair.

Don't hit people.

Put things back where you found them.

Clean up your own mess.

Don't take things that aren't yours.

Say you're sorry when you hurt somebody.

Wash your hands before you eat.

Flush.

Warm cookies and cold milk are good for you.

Live a balanced life – learn some and think some and draw and paint and sing and dance and play and work everyday some.

Take a nap every afternoon.

When you go out into the world, watch out for traffic, hold hands and stick together.

Wonder. Remember the little seed in the Styrofoam cup: the roots go down and the plant goes up and nobody really knows how or why, but we are all like that.

Goldfish and hamsters and white mice and even the little seed in the Styrofoam cup – they all die. So do we.

And then remember the *Dick and Jane* books and the first word you learned – the biggest word of all – LOOK.

Everything you need to know is in there somewhere. The Golden Rule and love and basic sanitation. Ecology and politics and equality and sane living.

Take any one of those items and extrapolate it into sophisticated adult terms and apply it to your family life or your work or your government or your world and it holds true and clear and firm. Think what a better world it would be if we all – the whole world – had cookies and milk about three o'clock every afternoon and then lay down with our blankies for a nap. Or if all governments had a basic policy to always put things back where they found them and to clean up their own mess.

And it is still true, no matter how old you are – when you go out into the world, it is best to hold hands and stick together.

Robert Fulghum

Reflections of a Parent

I gave you life,
But I cannot live it for you.
I can give you directions,
But I cannot be there to lead you.
I can take you to church,
But I cannot make you believe.
I can teach you right from wrong,
But I cannot always decide for you.
I can buy you beautiful clothes,
But I cannot make you beautiful inside.
I can offer you advice,
But I cannot accept it for you.
I can give you love,
But I cannot force it upon you.
I can teach you to share,
But I cannot make you unselfish.
I can teach you respect,
But I cannot force you to show honour.
I can advise you about friends,
But I cannot choose them for you.
I can advise you about sex,
But I cannot keep you pure.
I can tell you about alcohol and drugs,
But I cannot say 'no' for you.
I can tell you about lofty goals,
But I cannot achieve them for you.
I can teach you about kindness,
But I cannot force you to be gracious.
I can pray for you,
But I cannot make you walk with God.
I can tell you how to live,
But I cannot give you eternal life.
I can love you with unconditional love all my life …
And I will.

Author unknown

I Believe in Young People

I believe in young people when I see them rally together under a blazing sun to proclaim without fear the right of underdeveloped people to a just deal.

I believe in young people when I see them in the streets begging for alms to help evangelise the non-Christian world – and this not only on Missionary Days.

I believe in young people when I see them gathered around the altar of God, praying and meditating on the Scriptures.

I believe in young people when I see them casting their eyes beyond their immediate surroundings to consider the material and spiritual needs of so many people in this world.

I believe in young people when they do not show indifference to the sufferings of their fellow men.

I believe in young people when they face heat and cold in order to collect old clothes and books and suchlike things to help missionaries open new schools in a drive to eliminate illiteracy.

I believe in young people when they show grand ideals and then positively do something to help their needy fellow men.

I believe in young people when they speak out against over-spending and waste, and who at the same time keep their own expenditure at a minimum.

I believe in young people when they face up to their responsibilities as Christians and citizens and when they cut down on their own comforts so that the poor may benefit.

Author unknown

A Graduate's Prayer

Father, I have knowledge,
So will you show me now
How to use it wisely
And find a way somehow
To make the world I live in a better place,
And make life with its problems
A little bit easier to face.

Grant me faith and courage and put purpose in my days,
And show me how to serve thee
In the most effective ways.
So my education,
My knowledge and my skill
May find their true fulfilment
As I learn to do thy will.

And may I ever be aware
In everything I do,
That knowledge comes from learning,
And wisdom comes from you.

Amen.

Author unknown

Jesus the Teacher

He never taught a lesson in a classroom …
He had no tools to work with, no blackboards, maps or charts …
He used no subject outlines, kept no records, gave no grades,
and his only text was ancient and well worn.
His students were the poor, the lame, the deaf, the blind, the
outcast …
And his method was the same with all who came to hear and learn …
He opened eyes to faith …
He opened ears with simple truth …
And opened hearts with love, a love born of forgiveness …
A gentle man, a humble man,
He asked and won no honours, no gold awards of tribute to his
expertise or wisdom …
And yet this quiet teacher from the hills of Galilee has fed the needs,
Fulfilled the hopes, and changed the lives of many millions …
For what he taught, brought heaven to earth and God's heart to
mankind.

Author unknown

Ten Commandments for Students

1. I will come to school clean and tidy out of respect for myself and others.
2. I will do my homework so the day will be good for the teacher and for me.
3. I will behave quietly so I will not disturb the mental activity of others.
4. I will greet each fellow student with a smile and so spread God's joy to others.
5. I will obey all rules and regulations so good order will reign everywhere.
6. I will not be selfish and fail to help another when it's possible for me to help.
7. I will accept the hard work and discipline that study demands.
8. I will develop my mind so I can contribute to God's glory and to the good of others.
9. I will be grateful to teachers for their time and effort to help me learn more.
10. Each class will be seen as an opportunity to practice cooperation, consideration and respect.

Author unknown

Beatitudes for Teachers

Blessed are you who are called to teach, for you walk in the footsteps of the Master.

Blessed are you who sow peace and harmony in the staffroom, yours will be the joy of the Lord.

Blessed are you who plant seeds of hope in youthful hearts, for you will inherit the dawn.

Blessed are you who are sensitive to the cries of youth today, for they yearn for the coming of my Kingdom.

Blessed are you when you share your faith with others, for your name is written in my heart.

Blessed are you who anguish now because your students are difficult, one day they will thank you for your loving concern.

Blessed are you when efficiency is moderated by compassion and empathy, for the deeper secret of education is yours.

Blessed are you when you reach out to me in your students, for you will surely find me and rejoice.

Blessed are you who lead your young people in paths of justice and peace, for you will shine like stars for all eternity.

Author unknown

The Earth and Us

Reflection on Ecological Challenges

A solution to ecological challenges demands more than just economic and technological proposals. It requires an inner change of heart which leads to the rejection of unsustainable patterns of consumption and production. It demands an ethical behaviour which respects the principles of universal solidarity, social justice and responsibility.

Pope John Paul II, 27 May 2003

A Prayer for Sustainability

As we breathe the very air which sustains us,
we remember your love, God, which compels us.
Fill us with the spirit to seek understanding.
Empty us of apathy, selfishness and fear.
Fill us with compassion and generosity.
Empty us of all pessimism and hesitation.
Breathe into us solidarity with all who suffer
beneath the crossroads of pollution and poverty.
Breathe us into action building your sustainable Kingdom.
Hope.
We have only begun
to imagine the fullness of life.
How could we tire of hope?
… So much is in bud …
We have only begun to know
the power that is in us if we could join
our solitude in the communion of struggle.
So much is unfolding that must
complete its gesture.
So much is in bud.

Author unknown

The Beams of Love

'We are put on earth a little space,
That we might learn to bear the beams of love'
WILLIAM BLAKE

The beams of love are everywhere! This creation is God's love made visible! Stand near a tree. Look into the face of a flower or a field of wheat. Listen to a friend ... God's love is pulsing there. Visualise how God fills the empty spaces of each atom and the vast reaches of outer space. The world is full of love!

How did we ever come to think of earth as a place of exile rather than what it is – a wonderous garden of nourishment and beauty, where we are privileged to live? How could we have thought of ourselves as having to prove our worthiness to God, who loves us beyond measure already? The One who is everything we need and long for is already here!

And why have we made life such a big project? Why all the striving, the competition for power, for wealth, for things? Why the long hours of work, the stress, the violence against our own souls, against earth, one another?

If we looked at everything as if we were seeing it for the first time (or the last time, as dying persons attest), we would see life as pure gift, filled with glory! We would recognise the Generous One who is always giving birth to us and to our world – a soaring outflow of love and tender care. In God we live and move and have our being. What if we were to believe and live this?

What if I could put aside my striving and fear of others and realise that every person has the capacity to love and be loved? What if I saw every person of every nation relating to me, connected by common origin? What if I recognised all creatures as my brothers and sisters – all of us children of the God who is always moving within us and through us, weaving us into one precious fabric of life? What if we perceived the radiance within each other, just below the surface?

What joy would fill us if we could but see life for what it really is and is meant to be: 'sheer enjoyment and pure dancing in the spaciousness of love' (Gerald G. May) – an adventure in which we all participate! Growing in human hearts today is a new springtime of intelligence and awareness; one can imagine God dancing with delight and hope as we humans probe the mysteries of life, of the vast universe, of the tiny particles of the atom – and we recognise there the amazing interconnectedness of all creation! Will we get it now, after thousands of years of living the destructive illusion of separation?

We have only begun to imagine the depth and power of the love being poured forth at every moment – the wisdom, the heartbreaking beauty in which we are immersed. We have only begun to know ourselves, our human calling within the earth community, the love of which we too are capable. We can no longer claim to be lords and masters over the rest of creation, for now we know that we have been as young children, cared for by earth for millennia. Today we are called upon to put aside our self-absorbed ignorance and learn from earth how to partner her, to adopt her life-enhancing technologies which will heal, restore and promote life to the full.

And so we offer you this reflection that it may bear beams of love and hope to you throughout the year, and that falling into love, you may bear fruit – energies of love you'll learn to beam to others, and they in turn to others, and on and on in the great circle of life.

Author unknown

How to Build a Global Community

Think of no one as 'them'.
Don't confuse your comfort with your safety – talk to strangers.
Imagine other cultures through their poetry and novels.
Listen to music you don't understand; dance to it.
Act locally.
Notice the workings of power and privilege in your culture.
Question consumption.
Know how your lettuce and coffee are grown; wake up and smell the exploitation. Look for Fair Trade and Union labels.
Help build economies from the bottom up.
Acquire few needs.
Learn a second (or third) language.
Visit people, places, and cultures – not tourist attractions.
Learn people's history.
Re-define progress.
Know physical and political geography.
Play games from other cultures.
Watch films with subtitles.
Know your heritage.
Honour everyone's holidays.
Look at the moon and imagine someone else, somewhere else, looking at it too.
Read the UN's Universal Declaration of Human Rights.
Understand the global economy in terms of people, land and water.
Know where your bank banks.
Never believe you have a right to anyone else's resources.
Refuse to wear corporate logos: defy corporate domination.
Question military/corporate connections.
Don't confuse money with wealth, or time with money.
Have a pen/email pal.
Honour indigenous cultures.
Judge governance by how well it meets all people's needs.
Be sceptical about what you read.
Eat adventurously.
Enjoy vegetables, beans and grains in your diet.
Choose curiosity over certainty.
Know where your water comes from and where your wastes go.
Pledge allegiance to the earth: question nationalism.
Think South, Central and North – there are many Americans.

Assume that many others share your dreams.
Know that no one is silent though many are not heard – work to change this.

Syracuse Cultural Workers

Litany of the Circle

1. Every part of this earth is sacred.
   Every shining pine needle, every sandy shore.
2. Every mist in the dark woods.
   Every clearing and humming insect is holy.
3. The rocky crest, the juices of the meadow, the beasts and all the people.
   All belong to the same family.
4. Teach your children that the earth is our mother.
   Whatever befalls the earth befalls the children of the earth.
5. The water's murmur is the voice of our father's father.
   We are part of the earth, and the earth is part of us.
6. The rivers are our brothers; they quench our thirst.
   The perfumed flowers are our sisters.
7. The air is precious.
   For all of us share the same breath.
8. The wind that gave our grandparents breath also receives their last sign.
   The wind gave our children the spirit of life.
9. This we know, the earth does not belong to us.
   We belong to the earth.
10. This we know, all things are connected.
    Like the blood which unites one family.
11. All things are connected.
    Our God is the same God, whose compassion is equal for all.
12. For we did not weave the web of life.
    We are merely a strand in it.
13. Whatever we do to the web …
    We do to ourselves.
14. Let us give thanks for the web in the circle that connects us.
    Thanks be to God, the God of all.

Based on a speech by Chief Seattle, 1854

We Are the Earth

Earth is stardust come-to-life, a magic cauldron where the heart of the universe is being formed. In me, the earth and its creatures find their voices. Through my eyes, the stars look back on themselves in wonder.

I am the EARTH.

WE ARE THE AIR.
Air is the breath of the earth, the movement of life, the quick, violent storm and the slow, caressing breeze. In my breathing, life is received and given back. My breath unites me with all things, to the creatures that make the oxygen, and the people that share the same breath.

WE ARE FIRE.
Fire is the energy of the universe, the source of power and new life. In my thoughts burn the fires of eternal eruption of life, of emotions, lightning flashes. I participate in power. I share the energy of the universe, to keep warm, to fuel my body, to create my relationships.

I am FIRE. This is my power.

WE ARE WATER.
Water is the womb of the earth, from whom all life is born. The oceans flow through me, carrying food, recycling waste, expressing emotions.

I am WATER. This is my life.

What are you? What am I?

Response: Intersecting cycles of WATER, EARTH, AIR, FIRE. That's what I AM. That's what YOU ARE.

Daniel Martin

FOUR ELEMENTS MEDICINE WHEEL

O Great Spirit of the North
Invisible Spirit of the Air
And of the fresh, cool winds
O vast and boundless grandfather sky
Your living breath animates all life
Yours is the power of clarity and strength
Power to hear the inner sounds,
To sweep out the old patterns,
And to bring to change and challenge
The ecstasy of movement and the dance.
We pray that we may be aligned with you,
So that your power may flow through us, and be expressed by us
For the good of this planet,
And all living beings upon it.

O Great Spirit of the West,
Spirit of the Great Waters,
Of rain, rivers, lakes and springs.
O Grandmother Ocean
Deep matrix, womb of all life.
Power to dissolve boundaries,
To release holdings,
Power to taste and to feel,
To cleanse and to heal,
Great blissful darkness of peace.
We pray that we may be aligned with you,
So that your powers may flow through us,
And be expressed by us,
For the good of this planet,
And all living beings upon it.

O Great Spirit of the East,
Radiance of the rising Sun,
Spirit of new beginnings,
O Grandfather Fire, Great nuclear fire – of the Sun.
Power of life-energy, vital spark,
Power to see far, and to
Imagine with boldness.
Power to purify our senses,

Our hearts and our minds.
We pray that we may be aligned with you,
So that your powers may flow through us,
And be expressed by us,
For the good of this planet Earth,
And all living beings upon it.

O Great Spirit of the South,
Protector of the fruitful land,
And of all green and growing things,
The noble trees and grasses,
Grandmother Earth, Soul of Nature.
Great power of the receptive,
Of nurturance and endurance,
Power to grow and bring forth Flowers of the field,
Fruits of the garden.
We pray that we may be aligned with you,
So that your powers may flow through us,
And be expressed by us,
For the good of this planet Earth,
And all living beings upon it.

Ralph Metzner

The Ten Commandments of Ecology

1. I am the Lord your God who has created heaven and earth. Know that the earth is your mother and that you are a brother and sister to all creatures both living and non-living.
2. The earth is your mother who provides all your needs; therefore, love and cherish your mother not only for your own well-being but also for the well-being of your children, grandchildren and great-grand-children.
3. Know that you are part of the web of life. Therefore, take care that you do not destroy the web; otherwise, you also are destroyed.
4. Know that the earth does not belong to you; you belong to the earth. All creatures are connected with the genes that unite one family. All things are connected. Whatever befalls the earth befalls the children of the earth.
5. Love your Mother Earth in words and in deeds so that your children will do the same. See to it that there is credibility on your part.
6. Prevent the destruction of the forests, and the pollution of the air, water and soil by leading a simple lifestyle.
7. Be self-disciplined even in small details of your life. Avoid complacency.
8. Know that by your desire for wealth and your sophisticated lifestyle, you are destroying your mother, the planet earth. Allow your mother to become rich so that natural calamities may be minimised.
9. Know that when you were born you did not bring anything to this earth and when you die you will not be able to bring anything out. Therefore, be detached from all material things. Everything is transient such as wealth, prestige, power, even the human body.
10. Balance your spiritual life with your pursuit of livelihood. Set aside time for your weekly day of rest to be with the Lord and to be with the world, rather than use the world.

Sr Gloria A. Martires, SFIC

Earth Teach Me

Earth teach me stillness
as the grasses are stilled with light.
Earth teach me suffering
as old stones suffer with memory.
Earth teach me humility
as blossoms are humble with beginning.
Earth teach me caring
as the mother who secures her young.
Earth teach me courage
as the tree which stands alone.
Earth teach me limitation
as the ant which crawls on the ground.
Earth teach me freedom
as the eagle which soars in the sky.
Earth teach me resignation
as the leaves which die in the fall.
Earth teach me regeneration
as the seed which rises in the spring.
Earth teach me to forget myself
as melted snow forgets its life.
Earth teach me to remember kindness
as dry fields weep in the rain.

Ute prayer

Community and Interfaith

Blessing

May the blessing of PEACE fall upon us, peace in our hearts and peace in our homes, peace in our country and peace in our world. May the blessing of peace be ours.

May the blessing of HOPE fall upon us, hope in our pain and hope in our joy, hope for the poor and hope for the lonely, hope for those who are struggling and hope for those who have given up. May the blessing of hope be ours.

May the blessing of GOOD HEALTH fall upon us, health in our minds and in our emotions, health in our bodies and in our souls. May the blessing of good health be ours.

May the blessing of HAPPINESS fall upon us, happiness in our relationships and in our work, happiness in our decisions and in our memories. May the blessing of happiness be ours.

Author unknown

Mary, Queen of Peace

Mary, Queen of Peace,
we entrust our lives to you.
Shelter us from war, hatred
and oppression.

Teach us
to live in peace,
to educate ourselves for peace.
Inspire us to act justly,
to revere all God has made.
Root peace firmly in our hearts
and in our world.

Amen.

John Paul II

Modern Prayer for World Peace

Great God, who has told us
'Vengeance is mine',
save us from ourselves,
save us from the vengeance in our hearts,
and the acid in our souls.

Save us from our desire to hurt as we have been hurt,
to punish as we have been punished,
to terrorise as we have been terrorised.

Give us the strength it takes
to listen rather than to judge,
to trust rather than to fear,
to try again and again
to make peace even when peace eludes us.

We ask, O God, for the grace
to be our best selves.
We ask for the vision
to be builders of the human community
rather than its destroyers.
We ask for the humility as a people
to understand the fears and hopes of other peoples.
We ask for the love it takes
to bequeath to the children of the world to come
more than the failures of our own making.
We ask for the heart it takes
to care for all the peoples
of Afghanistan and Iraq, of Palestine and Israel
as well as for ourselves.

Give us the depth of soul, O God,
to constrain our might,
to resist the temptations of power,
to refuse to attack the attackable,
to understand that vengeance begets violence,
and to bring peace, not war, wherever we go.
For you, O God, have been merciful to us.

For you, O God, have been patient with us.
For you, O God, have been gracious to us.

And so may we be merciful
and patient
and gracious
and trusting
with these others whom you also love.
This we ask through Jesus,
the one without vengeance in his heart.
This we ask forever and ever. Amen

Sr Joan Chittister

On Being a Well

'You have no bucket, sir,' she answered, 'and the well is deep: how could you get this living water? Are you a greater man than our father Jacob who gave us this well and drank from it himself?' Jesus replied: 'Whoever drinks this water will get thirsty again; but anyone who drinks the water I shall give will never be thirsty again: the water that I shall give will turn into a spring inside him, welling up to eternal life.'

John 4:11-14

The first well I ever knew was our old family well at my childhood farm. Memories of drawing water from that well will stay with me forever. For the most part, my memories of drawing water are joyful ones. It is true, of course, that as a child I did not always go to the well willingly. Strange, how our hearts change. I would give anything today for a chance to go to that well and draw water for my family.

Although it may be too late to go to those childhood wells and draw water for our families in reality, it is never too late to do so in our memories. It is never too late to give a drink to the strangers in our families, even if the drink must be given symbolically. It is never too late to become a well for our thirsty sisters and brothers in all the families of this world. Nor is it too late to receive drinks from their wells.

There are wells hidden in the hearts of all the thirsty strangers we meet along the way. Sometimes, our honest search for living water can lead us to these wells, and exchanges can be made that quench our thirst.

After the woman at the well received her drink from Jesus, she became a well for others to drink from (Jn 4:39). In this meditation I want to challenge you to look for such wells along the way and to be such a well for others to find.

What makes this world so lovely
is that somewhere it hides a well.
Something lovely there is about a well
so deep
unpiped and real

filled
with buckets and buckets
of that life-giving drink.
A faucet will do in a hurry,
but what makes the world so lovely
is that somewhere
it hides a well!

Sometimes people are like wells
deep and real
natural (unpiped)
life-giving
calm and cool
refreshing.
They bring out what is best in you.
They are like fountains of pure joy.
They make you want to sing, or maybe dance.
They encourage you to laugh,
Even when things get rough.
And maybe that's why
things never stay rough once you've found a well.

Some experiences are like wells too.
People create them.
They are life-giving happenings.
They are redeeming experiences.
They are wells,
wells of wonder
wells of hope.

When you find a well
and you will some day,
drink deeply of the gift within.
And then maybe soon
you'll discover
that you've become
what you've received,
and then you'll be a well
for others to find.

So lift up your eyes
And look all around you:
over the mountains, down in the valley,
out in the ocean, over the runways,
into the cities, into the country,
sidewalks and highways,
paths in the forest,
into the hearts of thirsty people.

Look!
And I beg you
don't ever stop looking
because what makes this world so lovely
is that *somewhere*
it hides a well,
a well that hasn't been found yet.

And if you don't find it
maybe
nobody will!
And if you don't be one
maybe
nobody will find you!

Macrina Wiederkehr

How Can We?

How can we break bread
 and not remember those who have no bread?
How can we meet together
 and not remember those
 separated from their families and friends?
How can we shelter here
 and not remember those
 whose only shelter is a refugee camp or cardboard box?
How can we speak of peace
 and not remember those
 whose peace is shattered by constant fear and the rattle of guns?
How can we sing our hymns
 and not remember those
 who cannot openly express their religious beliefs?
How can we offer our gifts
 and not remember those
 who are caught in the never-ending cycle of poverty and debt?
How can we pour wine
 and not remember those
 who are imprisoned by addiction to bottle, needles or pills?
How can we celebrate
 and not remember those
 who suffer from depression, mental illness or grief?
God of human experience,
 born in a stable in Bethlehem,
Spirit alive in us today
 in our breaking of bread and pouring of wine,
 may we look outwards to the suffering of our world
 remembering the hope of your shalom.

Clare McBeath and Tim Presswood

A Conversational Prayer with the Woman Cured on the Sabbath

Luke 13:10-17

I am so glad your story did not get excluded when the patriarchal selectors decided to write women out of the Scripture to please the dominant political and social structure. I suppose you looked so harmless 'possessed by a spirit that drained your strength for eighteen years'. Surely you could not be a threat, and since your cure caused a clash with the synagogue, and brought Jesus one step nearer his death, maybe you might even share some of the blame for his death, just by being there. But you fooled them. For me you are like the tip of an iceberg above the water – for me you represent all the women bowed down by male domination and oppression for the past two thousand years, and still today. You are the great symbol of hope for us all, for Jesus says to you and to all oppressed women: 'Woman you are free of your infirmity.' He laid his hand on you and you stood up straight and began to thank God as a true 'daughter of Abraham'.

I see you in a very subversive memory. In Jesus you gained salvation, hope, an upright walk and a future. You can now look up and see the coming order. You have broken the bonds of the anxious, pragmatic, ecclesiastical solutions which Luke provides elsewhere. And you point to a Church of women and men who can stand upright, enjoying equal status. To you I address a litany of remembrance of some of the oppressions of our patriarchal world of the Church. To the battered and abused women bent down by injustice and oppression we say with Jesus: 'Stand up straight.'

To the forgotten women leaders of house churches in early Christianity –
Stand up straight.

To the valiant women buried and bent down by the weight of 2,000 years of history –
Stand up straight.

To the unnamed prophets and women leaders buried in the monument of patriarchy –
Stand up straight.

To our black sisters bowed down by centuries of slavery –
Stand up straight.

To the many women who have been 'used' –
Stand up straight.

To our Muslim sisters bowed down by a culture of oppression –
Stand up straight.

To the girl child in the man's world –
Stand up straight.

To the women who feel worthless and oppressed –
Stand up straight.

To the women who were raped, exploited, discriminated against and abused –
Stand up straight.

To women who are passed over, invisible and underpaid –
Stand up straight.

To women who are violated, excluded, harassed and ignored –
Stand up straight.

To all women trapped in a sexist society in a patriarchal world –
Stand up straight.

To all women shut off from a full life by traditional practice –
Stand up straight.

For those denied their freedom by systems and authority –
Stand up straight.

To women who labour too long and hard to barely feed their children –
Stand up straight.

To those women who lead lives of quiet desperation at the hands of the powerful and the prestigious –
Stand up straight.

To all women destroyed by persecution, whose bodies have been violated, whose spirits have been humiliated, who have been imprisoned and put to death –
Stand up straight.

REFLECTION

Many remarkable achievements are absent from the annals of history because they were done by women. And the conclusion is wrongly drawn that nothing was done by women, because nothing is recorded. We must keep women's memory alive, recall and recover her experiences, because all women are less visible, their collective worth less valuable when one woman disappears.

PRAYER

Help us to forgive those who perpetuate the patriarchal system, who foster misogynist values excluding us from sacred spaces, patronising us; help us to forgive those in professional spaces who monopolise and abuse power, pushing us towards despair and bending us down to the ground like the woman in the Gospel. And may we never be at peace while there is even a single one of us bowed down. Eternal sources of being give us the courage and the awareness to be able to say with conviction to all the oppressed of the earth: 'Stand up straight.'

Anne Holton

The Good

The good are vulnerable
As any bird in flight,
They do not think of safety,
Are blind to possible extinction
And when most vulnerable
Are most themselves.
The good are real as the sun,
Are best perceived through clouds
Of casual corruption
That cannot kill the luminous sufficiency
That shines on city, sea and wilderness,
Fastidiously revealing
One man to another,
Who yet will not accept
Responsibilities of light.
The good incline to praise,
To have the knack of seeing that
The best is not destroyed
Although forever threatened.
The good go naked in all weathers,
And by their nakedness rebuke
The small protective sanities
That hide men from themselves.
The good are difficult to see
Though open, rare, destructible;
Always, they retain a kind of youth,
The vulnerable grace
Of any bird in flight,
Content to be itself,
Accomplished master and potential victim,
Accepting what the earth or sky intends.
I think that I know one or two
Among my friends.

Brendan Kennelly

The Starfish

Once upon a time there was a man who used to go to the sea to do his writing. He had a habit of walking on the beach before he began work.

One day he was walking along the shore. Looking ahead, he saw a person moving like a dancer. He smiled to himself, thinking warmly of someone dancing to the day. So he began to walk faster to catch up.

As he got closer, he saw that it was a young man and he wasn't dancing, but instead reaching down to the sand, picking up something and very gently throwing it in the sea.

As he got closer he called out, 'Good morning! What are you doing?'

The young man looked up and replied, 'Throwing starfish in the sea.'

'I suppose I should have asked, "Why are you throwing starfish in the sea?"'

'The sun is up, and the tide is going out. And if I don't throw them in they'll die.'

'But don't you realise that there are miles and miles of beach with starfish all along it? You can't possibly make a difference!'

The young man listened politely. Then bent down, picked another starfish and threw it into the sea, past the breaking waves and said, 'It made a difference to that one.'

Author unknown

A Sleep of Prisoners

Dark and cold we may be, but this
Is no winter now. The frozen misery
Of centuries breaks, cracks, begins to move;
The thunder is the thunder of the floes,
The thaw, the flood, the upstart Spring.
Thank God our time is now when wrong
Comes up to face us everywhere,
Never to leave us till we take
The longest stride of soul we ever took.
Affairs are now soul size.
The enterprise
Is exploration into God.
Where are you making for? It takes
So many thousand years to wake,
But will you wake for pity's sake!

Christopher Fry

The Restless Heart

IT WAS A COLD, DARK THURSDAY NIGHT,
A man was discouraged,
Discouraged as only one could be,
Who looks on much hard work,
on much sincerity
and sees only failure,
and a sinking sun.

IT WAS A COLD, DARK THURSDAY NIGHT,
A man feels alone,
and lonely,
and frightened.
He sweats blood, in darkness,
the blood of loneliness,
the loneliness of all people.

ON THAT DARK THURSDAY NIGHT,
A man looked on loneliness, and
He yearned to heal.
He yearned to lead all into unity,
Into Community, and
Out of the damned aloneness
Which keeps people from warmth and life.

ON THAT DARK THURSDAY NIGHT,
A man sweats blood,
in body and spirit.
He sweats in darkness,
He sweats in loneliness,
And
it is then …

ON THAT DARK THURSDAY NIGHT,
A man takes his bread and wine, and says:
'This is my body, this is my blood,
Meet often,
Eat this bread, drink this wine,
And when you do,
I'll be there, and …

AS ON THIS DARK THURSDAY NIGHT,
I'll be leading you out of fear and loneliness,
Out of isolation and darkness.
Into Communion,
Into a Community of warmth and life,
with God, and
with each other.'

ON ONE DARK THURSDAY NIGHT,
When the sun had long gone down,
And hope and warmth had said goodbye,
When the darkness of loneliness had seemed to win the earth,
We were given,
as a gift from God,
the possibility of Community.

Ronald Rolheiser

Kate's Poem

What do you see nurse? What do you see?
What are you thinking when you're looking at me?

A crabbed old woman, not very wise,
Uncertain of habit, with far away eyes,
Who dribbles her food, and makes no reply,
When you say in a loud voice, 'I do wish you'd try!'
Who seems not to notice the things that you do,
And forever is losing a stocking or a shoe!
Who unresisting or not, lets you do as you will,
While bathing or breathing, the long day to fill.

Is that what you're thinking? Is that what you see?
Then open your eyes nurse, you're not looking at me.

I'll tell you who I am as I sit here so still,
As I do at your biding, as I eat at your will.

I'm a small child of ten, with a father and mother,
Brothers and sisters who love one another.

A young girl of sixteen with wings on her feet,
Dreaming that soon a new lover she'll meet.

To arrive soon at twenty, my heart gives a leap
Remembering the vows that I've promised to keep.

I'm twenty-five now, I have young of my own.
Who need me to build a secure, happy home.

A woman of thirty, my young now grow fast.
Bound to each other with ties that will last.

At forty, my young son's grown, and soon will be gone.
But my man stays beside me to see I don't mourn.

At fifty, babies once more play round my knee.
Again we know children, my loved one and me.

Dark days are upon me, my husband is dead.
I look to the future, I shudder with dread.
For my young are all busy, raising young of their own.
And I think of the years and the love I have known.

I'm an old woman now and nature is cruel.
To suggest, to make old age look like a fool.
The body it crumbles, grace and vigour dispelled,
But inside this old carcass a young girl still dwells.

I remember the joys, I remember the pain
And I'm loving and living life over again.
I think of the years, all too few, gone too fast.
And accept the stark fate, that nothing can last.

So open your eyes nurse; open and see,
Not a crabbed old woman. Look closer, see me!

Kate was a pensioner unable to speak. This poem was found in her locker after her death.

Colours

Once upon a time, the colours in the world started to quarrel: all claimed that they were the best, the most important, the most useful, the favourite.

Green said: 'Clearly, I am the most important. I am the sign of life and of hope. I was chosen for grass, trees, leaves – without me, all the animals would die.'

Blue interrupted: 'Consider the sky and the sea. It is the water that is the basis of life and the sky gives space and peace and serenity.'

Yellow chuckled: 'I bring laughter, gaiety and warmth into the world. The sun is yellow, the moon is yellow, the stars are yellow. Every time you look at a sunflower, the whole world starts to smile.'

Orange started next to blow her own trumpet: 'I am the colour of health and strength. Think of carrots and oranges, mangoes, and papayas. When I fill the sky at sunrise or sunset, no one gives another thought to any of you.'

Red could stand it no longer. He shouted out: 'I am the ruler of you all – life's blood! I am the colour of danger and of bravery. I am the colour of passion and of love.'

Purple rose up to his full height: 'I am the colour of royalty and power. Kings, chiefs and bishops have always chosen me for I am a sign of authority and wisdom.'

Indigo spoke much more quietly than all the others: 'Think of me. I am the colour of silence. I represent thought and reflection, twilight and deep waters. You need me for prayer and for peace.'

And so the colours went on boasting. Suddenly there was a startling flash of bright lightening: thunder rolled and boomed. Rain started to pour down relentlessly. The colours all crouched down in fear, drawing close to one another for comfort.

Then the rain spoke: 'You foolish colours, fighting amongst yourselves, each trying to dominate the rest. Do you not know that God made you all? Each made for a special purpose, unique and different? He loves you all. Join hands with one another and come with me. He will stretch you across the sky in a great bow of colour as a reminder that he loves you all, that you can live together in peace – a sign of hope for tomorrow.'

And so, whenever God has used a good rain to wash the world, he puts the rainbow in the sky, and when we see it, let us remember to appreciate one another.

Based on a Native American legend

The Face of God

A newspaper photographer was sent to Ecuador in 1987 to cover the earthquake that devastated much of the country. In the midst of such catastrophic suffering, he witnessed a simple scene of compassion.

The line was long but moving briskly. And in that line, at the very end, stood a young girl about twelve years of age. She waited patiently as those at the front of that long line received a little rice, some canned goods or a little fruit. Slowly but surely she was getting closer to the front of that line, closer to the food.

From time to time she would glance across the street. She did not notice the growing concern on the faces of those distributing the food. The food was running out. Their anxiety began to show, but she did not notice. Her attention seemed always to focus on three figures under the trees across the street.

At long last she stepped forward to get her food. But the only thing left was a lonely banana.

The workers were almost ashamed to tell her that was all that was left.

She did not seem to mind getting that solitary banana. Quietly she took the precious fruit and ran across the street where three small children waited – perhaps her sisters and a brother.

Very deliberately she peeled the banana and carefully divided it into three equal parts.

Placing the precious food into the eager hands of those three younger ones – one for you, one for you, one for you – she then sat down and licked the inside of the banana peel.

In that moment, I swear I saw the face of God.

Author unknown

Our First Task

Our first task in approaching
another people
another culture
another religion
is to take off our shoes,
for the place we are approaching is holy.
As we may find ourselves
treading on another's dream.
More serious still, we may forget …
that God was there
before we arrived.

Brigid O'Hara and Ellen Fleming

The Great Prayer of Islam

This prayer is called the Fatiha, i.e. the 'Opening' of the Qur'an, of which it is the first chapter.

In the name of God, the Compassionate, the Merciful
Praise be to God, Lord of the Creation,
The Compassionate, the Merciful,
King of Judgement Day!
You alone we worship, and to you alone we pray for help.
Guide us to the straight path
The path of those whom you have favoured,
Not of those who have incurred your wrath,
Nor of those who have gone astray.

The Rabbi's Gift

There was a famous monastery which had fallen on very hard times. Formerly its many buildings were filled with young monks and its big church resounded with the singing of the chant, but now it was deserted. People no longer went there to be nourished by prayer. A handful of old monks shuffled through the cloisters and praised their God with heavy hearts.

On the edge of the monastery woods, an old rabbi had built a little hut. He would go there from time to time to fast and pray. No one ever spoke with him, but whenever he appeared, the word would be passed from monk to monk: 'The rabbi walks in the woods.' And, for as long as he was there, the monks would feel sustained by his prayerful presence.

One day the abbot decided to visit the rabbi and to open his heart to him. So, after the morning Eucharist, he set out through the woods. As he approached the hut, the abbot saw the rabbi standing in the doorway, his arms outstretched in welcome. It was as though he had been waiting there sometime. The two embraced like long-lost brothers. Then they stepped back and just stood there, smiling broadly at one another.

After a while the rabbi motioned the abbot to enter. In the middle of the room was a wooden table with the Scriptures open on it. They sat there for a moment, in the presence of the Book. Then the rabbi began to cry. The abbot could not contain himself. He covered his face with his hands and began to cry too. For the first time in his life, he cried his heart out. The two men sat there like lost children, filling the hut with their sobs and wetting the wood of the table with their tears.

After the tears had ceased to flow and all was quiet again, the rabbi lifted his head. 'You and your brothers are serving God with heavy hearts,' he said. 'You have come to ask a teaching of me. I will give you a teaching, but you can repeat it only once. After that, no one must ever say it aloud again.'

The rabbi looked straight at the abbot and said, 'The Messiah is among you.' For a while, all was silent. The rabbi said, 'Now you must go.'

The abbot left without a word and without ever looking back. The next morning, the abbot called his monks together in the chapter room. He told them he had received a teaching from the 'rabbi who walks in the woods' and that this teaching was never again to be spoken aloud. Then he looked at each of his brothers and said, 'The rabbi said that one of us is the Messiah.'

The monks were startled by this saying. 'What could it mean?' they asked themselves. 'Is Brother John the Messiah? Or Brother Matthew or Brother Thomas? Am I the Messiah? What could all this mean?' They were all deeply puzzled by the rabbi's teaching, but no one ever mentioned it again.

As time went by, the monks began to treat one another with a very special reverence. There was a gentle, wholehearted, human quality about them now which was hard to describe but easy to notice. They lived with one another as men who had finally found something. But they prayed the Scriptures together as men who were always looking for something. Occasional visitors found themselves deeply moved by the life of these monks. Before long, people were coming from far and wide to be nourished by the prayer life of the monks, and young men were asking, once again, to become a part of the community.

After that, the rabbi no longer walked in the woods. His hut fell into ruins. But, somehow or other, the old monks who had taken his teaching to heart still felt sustained by his wise and prayerful presence.

Author unknown

A Dream for Europe

Based on Isaiah 11:1-10

New shoots will spring up
from the withered tree of Europe.
A new community will rise out of its roots.
The Spirit of the Lord will rest upon it,
a spirit of wisdom and moderation, a spirit of tolerance.
Its judgement will not depend
on the price of stocks and shares,
they will not be made at the behest of bankers.
Young people will be given reasons to hope,
and the weak the chance to make choices.
Its treaties will be inspired by justice.
Ethnic groups will live side by side
without fearing the loss of their identity.
Refugees will be safe in their new homes,
immigrants will no longer suffer aggression.
Catholic and Orthodox will discover evangelism together,
a woman pastor will guide them,
a young Muslim will invite them to celebrate Ramadan.
Fields of corn will no longer declare war on hedgerows,
pine and beech will flourish side by side,
Otters will populate the rivers again,
for no longer will anybody say 'it's not profitable'.
The South will not be destroyed
for the pleasure of the North,
for the knowledge of the Lord will fill the continent,
like the waters of the sea becoming clear again.

Pax Christi International, Brussels

A Priest

To live in the midst of the world
without wishing its pleasures;
To be a member of each family,
yet belonging to none;
To share all suffering,
to penetrate all secrets;
To heal all wounds;
To go from men to God
and offer him their prayers;
To return from God to men
to bring pardon and hope;
To have a heart of fire for Charity,
and a heart of bronze for Chastity;
To teach and to pardon,
console and bless always.
My God, what a life;
And it is yours,
O priest of Jesus Christ.

Lacordaire

Make Me an Instrument of Your Peace

St Francis of Assisi, with his profound sense of God's hand at the heart of creation, had first-hand experience of and a deep regard for Islam. In many ways he is a suitable patron for interfaith. The ideal expressed in this prayer speaks of the practical attitudes of respect and reconciliation which are needed if God's peace is to be channelled to a suffering humanity.

Lord, make me an instrument of your peace.
Where there is hatred, let me sow love.
Where there is injury, pardon.
Where there is doubt, faith.
Where there is despair, hope.
Where there is darkness, light.
Where there is sadness, joy.

O Divine Master,
grant that I may not so much seek
to be consoled as to console;
to be understood, as to understand;
to be loved as to love.
For it is in giving that we receive.
It is in pardoning that we are pardoned,
and it is in dying that we are born to eternal life.

Attributed to St Francis of Assisi

A Better Self

The Optimist Creed

To be so strong that nothing that happens can disturb your peace of mind.

To talk health, happiness and prosperity to every person you meet.

To make all your friends feel that there is something in them.

To look at the sunny side of everything and make your optimism come true.

To think only of the best, to work only for the best, and to expect only the best.

To be just as enthusiastic about the success of others as you are about your own.

To forget the mistakes of the past and press on to the greater achievements of the future.

To wear a cheerful countenance at all times and give every living creature you meet a smile.

To give so much time to the improvement of yourself that you have no time to criticise others.

To be too large for worry, too noble for anger, too strong for fear, and too happy to allow the presence of trouble.

To think well of yourself and to proclaim this fact to the world, not in loud words but in great deeds.

To live in the faith that the whole world is on your side so long as you are true to the best in you.

Christian Daa Larson

The Man Who Thinks He Can

If you think you are beaten, you are;
If you think you dare not, you don't.
If you'd like to win, but think you can't
It's almost a cinch you won't.
If you think you'll lose, you've lost.
For out in the world we find
Success begins with a fellow's will;
It's all in the state of mind.

If you think you're outclassed, you are;
You've got to think high to rise.
You've got to be sure of yourself before
You can ever win a prize.
Life's battles don't always go
To the stronger or faster man;
But soon or late the man who wins
Is the one who thinks he can.

Walter D. Wintle

Twenty Truths to Remember

1. Faith is the ability to not panic.
2. If you worry, you didn't pray. If you prayed, don't worry.
3. As a child of God, prayer is kind of like calling home every day.
4. Blessed are the flexible, for they shall not be bent out of shape.
5. When we get tangled up in our problems, be still. God wants us to be still so he can untangle the knot.
6. Do the math. Count your blessings.
7. Nothing is real to you until you experience it, otherwise it's only hearsay.
8. Dear God: I have a problem. It's me!
9. Silence is often misinterpreted, but never misquoted.
10. Laugh every day, it's like inner jogging.
11. The most important things in your home are the people.
12. Learn from the turtle … it only makes progress when it sticks out its neck.
13. There is no key to happiness. The door is always open.
14. A grudge is a heavy thing to carry.
15. He who dies with the most toys is still dead.
16. We do not remember days, but moments. Life moves too fast, so enjoy your precious moments.
17. God wants us to be spiritual fruit, not religious nuts.
18. It's all right to sit on your pity pot every now and again. Just be sure to flush when you're done.
19. Growing old is inevitable, growing up is optional.
20. Be more concerned with your character than your reputation. Your character is what you really are while your reputation is merely what others think you are.

Author unknown

To Live Truly, Freely

To live truly, fully, freely
God, you are the Giver of Life.
The whole universe has its being only as a gift of your love.
In communion with all created things I stand in awe and wonder before this great mystery of life.

I see that all creation
– trees, birds, stones, mice, seas, mountains –
gives glory and thanks to you
just by being what they are
and taking their part in the unfolding of the universe story.
However long or short their span of life, each has its part to play.

I believe now that my destiny is for me too,
to live fully what I am,
and in this way give thanks and praise for the wonder of my being,
and so reflect your beauty and truth in the world.

Help me to participate in the story of life
by being responsible and loving my relationship with all creation:
not as a superior being, not taking more than I need,
not seeking to dominate or make myself the centre of everything,
not being manipulative, blind, demanding, controlling,
or interfering with the ongoing process of creation.

Help me rather to welcome differences,
difficulties and sacrifices, losses, uncertainties, tensions and even death
as part of the natural conditions for growth and the emergence of new life.

Lord, the deepest desire of my heart
is to live truly, fully and freely as you made me.
So often I lose sight of this;
I live falsely and am not present to what is unfolding around and within me.

Help me to be more aware,
to see more clearly what your dream is for me,
to respond lovingly, freely and generously to your invitation –
drawing me more and more deeply into eternal union
with all that is
and with you, my loving God.

Margaret Rose McSparran, CP

Dream Dreams

The Lord gathers us into his kingdom
That we may know the love and glory
of the Father.

Dreams come and go in our lives.
Far more die than come to reality.

What is it in us that allows us to let
go of visions that could create new
and beautiful worlds?

Why do we let ourselves conform and be
satisfied with what is?

Reaching out to a dream can be risky.
It can involve hardships that our
imaginations never knew.
Our comfortableness can so easily be
disturbed.

But, what beauty can be experienced as we
accept the challenge of a dream.
What a precious feeling to be supported,
to have others say you can do it,
we can do it together.

Nothing is beyond our reach if we
reach out together,
If we reach out with all the confidence
we have.

If we are willing to persevere even in
difficult times
And if we rejoice with every small step forward,
If we dream beautiful dreams that will
transform our lives, our world.

Nothing is impossible
    if we put aside our careful ways,
    if we build our dreams with faith –
    faith in ourselves,
    faith in our sisters and brothers,
    and above all,
    faith in our Lord God
    with whom all things are possible.

All: Lord, the more we dream, the farther our hopes will take us. Let us be carried on the wings of our dreams with a confidence yet unknown. May we accept our challenges with unfounded enthusiasm, for nothing is impossible in your midst. Let us be blind to obstacles and limitations as we build your glorious kingdom. We ask this through Christ, our Lord.
Amen.

Debra Hintz

Fast and Feast

Fast from judging others; feast on the Christ dwelling within them.
Fast from emphasis on differences; feast on the unity of all life.
Fast from apparent darkness; feast on the reality of light.
Fast from words that pollute; feast on phrases that purify.
Fast from discontent; feast on gratitude.
Fast from anger; feast on patience.
Fast from pessimism; feast on optimism.
Fast from worry; feast on trust.
Fast from complaining; feast on appreciation.
Fast from negatives; feast on affirmatives.
Fast from unrelenting pressures; feast on unceasing prayer.
Fast from hostility; feast on non-violence.
Fast from bitterness; feast on forgiveness.
Fast from self-concern; feast on compassion for others.
Fast from personal anxiety; feast on eternal truth.
Fast from discouragement; feast on hope.
Fast from facts that depress; feast on truths that uplift.
Fast from lethargy; feast on enthusiasm.
Fast from suspicion; feast on truth.
Fast from thoughts that weaken; feast on promises that inspire.
Fast from idle gossip; feast on purposeful silence.

William Arthur Ward

You Are Blessed

Strange that Jesus says that we are blessed
if we are poor, gentle, mourning, merciful, peacemakers.
Others might say we are blessed
if we are rich, tough and comfortable,
and looking for our own rights and desserts.

There is a blessing in all that he says:
not an immediate happiness or prosperity,
but a blessing that comes from God
in the times when we are weak, vulnerable, broken.

The bread of the Eucharist is bread broken and shared,
the blessing of God is mourning accepted and shared;
the blessing of God is mercy asked and given
so that the bread of the Eucharist is the bread of forgiveness;
and the blessing of God fills the places of the soul
where I am poor, lost, gentle,
and willing to let go of the grudges of life
for the resurrection of Jesus.

Author unknown

Beatitudes Explained

Blessed are the poor in spirit,
not the penniless
but those whose heart is free
for theirs is the kingdom of heaven.

Blessed are those who mourn
not those who whimper
but those who raise their voices
for they shall be comforted.

Blessed are the meek
not the soft
but those who are patient and tolerant
for they will inherit the earth.

Blessed are those who hunger and thirst for righteousness
not those who whine
but those who struggle with fire in their bellies to see right prevail
for they will be filled.

Blessed are the merciful
not those who forget
but those who forgive.
for they will receive mercy.

Blessed are the pure in heart
not those who act like angels
but those whose life is transparent
for they will see God.

Blessed are the peacemakers
not those who shun conflict
but those who face it squarely
for they will be called children of God.

Blessed are those who are persecuted for righteousness' sake
not because they suffer
but because they love
for theirs is the kingdom of heaven.

Adapted from Compartir, Chile

Anyway

People are often unreasonable, illogical
and self-centred;
Forgive them anyway.

If you are kind, people may accuse you
of selfish, ulterior motives;
Be kind anyway.

If you are successful, you will win some
false friends and some true enemies;
Succeed anyway.

If you are honest and frank,
people may cheat you;
Be honest and frank anyway.

What you spend years building,
someone could destroy overnight;
Build anyway.

If you find serenity and happiness,
they may be jealous;
Be happy anyway.

The good you do today,
people will often forget tomorrow;
Do good anyway.

Give the world the best you have,
and it may never be enough;
Give the world the best you've got anyway.

You see, in the final analysis,
it is between you and your God;
It was never between you and them anyway.

Attributed to Mother Teresa

Life

Life is an opportunity, benefit from it.
Life is beauty, admire it.
Life is bliss, taste it.
Life is a dream, realise it.
Life is a challenge, meet it.
Life is a duty, complete it.
Life is a game, play it.
Life is costly, care for it.
Life is wealth, keep it.
Life is love, enjoy it.
Life is mystery, know it.
Life is a promise, fulfill it.
Life is sorrow, overcome it.
Life is a song, sing it.
Life is a struggle, accept it.
Life is tragedy, confront it.
Life is an adventure, dare it.
Life is luck, make it.
Life is too precious, do not destroy it.
Life is life, fight for it.

Attributed to Mother Teresa

Indispensable

Some time when you're feeling important,
Some time when your ego's in bloom,
Some time when you take it for granted
You're the best qualified man in the room;
Some time when you think that your going
Would leave an unfillable hole,
Just follow these simple instructions
And see how they humble your soul:
Take a bucket and fill it with water,
Put your hand in it up to your wrist,
Pull it out and the hole that remains
Is the measure of how you'll be missed.
You may splash as you please when you enter,
You may stir up the waters galore,
But stop – and you'll find in a minute
That it looks just the same as before.
The moral of this is quite simple:
Do just the best that you can,
Be proud of yourself, but remember:
There is no indispensable man.

Author unknown

A Blessing of Solitude

May you recognise in your life the presence, power, and light of your soul.
May you realise that you are never alone,
that your soul in its brightness and belonging connects you intimately with the rhythm of the universe.
May you have respect for your own individuality and difference.
May you realise that the shape of your soul is unique, that
you have a special destiny here,
that behind the facade of your life there is something
beautiful, good, and eternal happening.
May you learn to see yourself with the same delight, pride,
and expectation with which God sees you in every moment.

John O'Donohue

A Blessing

May the light of your soul guide you.
May the light of your soul bless the work you do with the secret love and warmth of your heart.
May you see in what you do the beauty of your own soul.
May the sacredness of your work bring healing, light, and renewal to those who work with you and to those who see and receive your work.
May your work never weary you.
May it release within you wellsprings of refreshment, inspiration, and excitement.
May you be present in what you do.
May you never become lost in the bland absences.
May the day never burden.
May dawn find you awake and alert, approaching your new day with dreams, possibilities, and promises.
May evening find you gracious and fulfilled.
May you go into the night blessed, sheltered, and protected.
May your soul calm, console, and renew you.

John O'Donohue

Beginners

But we have only begun
To love the earth.

We have only begun
To imagine the fullness of life.

How could we tire of hope?
– so much is in bud.

How can desire fail?
– we have only begun

to imagine justice and mercy,
only begun to envision

how it might be
to live as siblings with beast and flower,
not as oppressors.

Surely our river
cannot already be hastening
into the sea of nonbeing?

Surely it cannot
drag, in the silt,
all that is innocent?

Not yet, not yet –
there is too much broken
that must be mended,

too much hurt we have done to each other
that cannot yet be forgiven.

We have only begun to know
the power that is in us if we would join
our solitudes in the communion of struggle.

So much is unfolding that must
complete its gesture,

so much is in bud.

Denise Levertov

A Creed to Live By

Don't undermine your worth
By comparing yourself with others.
It is because we are different
That each of us is special.
Don't set your goals by what
Other people deem important.
Only do what is best for you.
Don't take for granted the things
Closest to your heart.
Cling to them as you would your life –
For without them life is meaningless.
Don't let life slip through your fingers
By living in the past or in the future.
By living your life one day at a time,
You live all days of your life.
Don't give up when you still have something to give.
Nothing is really over
Until the moment you stop trying.
Don't be afraid to admit that you are less than perfect.
It is the fragile thread that binds us to each other.
Don't be afraid to encounter risks –
It is by taking chances that we learn how to be brave.
Don't shut love out of your life
By saying it is impossible to find.
The quickest way to receive love
Is to give love.
The fastest way to keep love
Is to give it wings.
Don't dismiss your dreams.
To be without dreams is to be without hope.
To be without hope is to be without purpose.
Don't run through life so fast
That you forget not only where you have been,
But also where you are going.
Life is not a race, but a journey to be savoured
Each step of the way.

Nancye Sims

Workers, Not Master Builders

It helps, now and then, to step back and take the long view. The kingdom is not only beyond our efforts, it is beyond our vision.

We accomplish in our lifetime only a tiny fraction of the magnificent enterprise that is God's work. Nothing we do is complete, which is another way of saying that the kingdom always lies beyond us. No statement says all that could be said. No prayer fully expresses our faith. No confession brings perfection. No pastoral visit brings wholeness. No programme accomplishes the Church's mission. No set of goals and objectives includes everything.

This is what we are about. We plant seeds that one day will grow. We water seeds already planted, knowing that they hold future promise. We lay foundations that will need further development. We provide yeast that produces effects beyond our capabilities.

We cannot do everything, and there is a sense of liberation in realising that. This enables us to do something, and do it very well. It may be incomplete, but it's a beginning, and a step along the way, an opportunity for the Lord's grace to enter and do the rest.

We may never see the end results, but that is the difference between the master builder and the worker.

We are workers, not master builders; ministers, not messiahs. We are prophets of a future not our own.
Amen.

Archbishop Oscar Romero

I Am Special

I am special. In all the world there's nobody like me. Since the beginning of time, there has been no one like me. Nobody has my smile. Nobody has my eyes, my nose, my hands, my voice. I'm special. No one can be found who has my handwriting. Nobody anywhere has my tastes – for food, music or art. No one sees just as I do. In all of time there's been no one who laughs like me, no one who cries like me. And what makes me laugh and cry will never provoke identical laughter and tears from anybody else, ever.

No one responds to any situation just as I would respond. I'm special. I'm the only one in all of creation who has my set of abilities. Oh, there will always be somebody who is better at one of the things I'm good at, but no one in the universe can reach the quality of my combination of talents, ideas, abilities and feelings. Like a room full of musical instruments, some may excel alone, but none can match the symphony sound when all are played together. I'm not a symphony.

Through all of eternity no one will ever look, talk, walk, think or do like me. I'm special. I'm rare. And in all rarity there is great value. Because of my great rare value, I need not attempt to imitate others. I will accept – yes, celebrate – my differences.

I'm special. And I'm beginning to realise it's no accident that I'm special. I'm beginning to see that God made me special for a very special purpose. He must have a job for me that no one else can do.

I'm special.
My child, you are precious in my eyes.
And I love you.
(God, my Father).
Father, Son, and Holy Spirit, I adore you, I love you, and I thank you for the wonder of my being the miracle of your presence in me.

Author unknown

MEDITATION ON ONE'S INDIVIDUAL GIFT

Every pot made on a wheel is the evolution of a lump of clay. The clay grows into a pot by the distinctive method of throwing. For this reason, it is difficult to achieve a unique factory-made pot. Liquid clay is poured into identical moulds so the resulting pots are identical. They are perfect, if perfect means being no different from the rest. It's an inhuman kind of perfection. Mass-produced pottery is seldom attractive or interesting. But handmade pots often have great charm and they always have at least the charm of individuality. They can be more or less alike but never identical, never perfect imitations. In museums you can see hand-thrown pots that are several thousand years old and still bearing the fingerprints of the potter who made them.

I often wished that I were different, that I looked different from the way I look, that I had a different history, different gifts, other people's gifts usually. When I try to change, luckily my efforts are not always successful – luckily, because what I try to change may well be a gift in disguise. God often prevents me from throwing away the things of real value in my life. Some things I can never change no matter how much I try – my age for instance, or the facts of my history, or the deepest core of my identity.

God loves me as I am, I say, but I am seldom what I am. I am a hundred different people. My name is legion. I am a stranger to the deepest core of my identity, so I go looking for identity in the wrong direction. I question other people's faces to tell me who I am and they give me a predictable answer. I am one of them if I am like them in every way, so then my identity would lie in imitating them – then I have individuality.

There is a deep boredom. I am mass-produced – like factory pottery. Instead I need to have the courage of the individual gifts the Lord has placed in me.

I need to value the shape that his providence has given to my life. My life is an individual creation and bears God's fingerprints. Lord, I am like one who holds a treasure but doesn't know its value. I place myself here in your presence, an earthen vessel, individual, imperfect. Let me catch a glimpse of my true self, the self that comes from your hand; then I will be free of envy and imitation and the craving for altered circumstances. Let me see clearly in the practice of my life that the deepest changes are at the heart's core.

Author unknown

The Cracked Pot

A water bearer in India had two large pots, one hung on each end of a pole which he carried across his neck.

One of the pots had a crack in it. The other pot was perfect and always delivered a full portion of water at the end of the long walk from the stream to the master's house, but the cracked pot arrived only half full. For over two years this went on daily, with the bearer delivering only one and a half pots full of water to his master.

Of course, the perfect pot was proud of its achievements, perfect to the end for which it was made. But the poor cracked pot was ashamed of its own imperfection, and miserable that it was able to accomplish only half of what it had been made to do.

After two years of what it thought of as bitter failure, the cracked pot spoke to the water bearer one day by the stream. 'I am ashamed of myself, and I want to apologise to you.'

'Why?' asked the bearer. 'What are you ashamed of?'

'I have been able, for these past two years, to deliver only half my load because this crack in my side causes water to leak out all the way back to your master's house. Because of my flaws, you have to do more journeys, and you don't get full value from your efforts,' the pot said.

The water bearer felt sorry for the old cracked pot, and said, 'As we return to the master's house, I want you to notice the beautiful flowers along the path.'

Indeed, as they went up the hill, the old cracked pot took notice of the sun warming the beautiful wild flowers on the side of the path, and this cheered it a little. But at the end of the trail, it still felt bad because it had leaked out half its load, and so again the pot apologised to the bearer for its failure.

The bearer said to the pot, 'Did you notice that there were flowers only on your side of the path, but not on the other pot's side? That's because I have always known about your flaw, and I took advantage of it. I planted flower seeds on your side of the path, and every day while we walk back from the stream, you've watered them. For two years I have been able to pick these beautiful flowers to decorate my master's table. Without you being just the way you are, he would not have this beauty to grace his house.'

Each of us has our own unique flaws. We're all cracked pots. But if we will allow it, God will use our flaws to a good purpose. In God's great economy, nothing goes to waste. Don't be afraid of your flaws.

Acknowledge them, and you too can be the cause of beauty. It's so often in our weakness that we find our strength.

Author unknown

The Woodcarver

Khing, the master carver, made a bell stand
Of precious wood. When it was finished,
All who saw it were astounded. They said it must be
The work of spirits.
The Prince of Lu said to the master carver:
'What is your secret?'

Khing replied: 'I am only a workman:
I have no secret. There is only this:
When I began to think about the work you commanded
I guarded my spirit, did not expend it
On trifles that were not to the point.
I fasted in order to set
My heart at rest.
After three days fasting,
I had forgotten gain and success.
After five days I had forgotten praise or criticism.
After seven days I had forgotten my body
With all its limbs.

'By this time all thought of your Highness
And of the court had faded away.
All that might distract me from the work
Had vanished.
I was collected in the single thought
Of the bell stand.

'Then I went to the forest
To see the trees in their own natural state.
When the right tree appeared before my eyes,
The bell stand also appeared in it, clearly, beyond doubt.
All I had to do was to put forth my hand
and begin.

'If I had not met this particular tree
There would have been
No bell stand at all.

'What happened?
My own collected thought
Encountered the hidden potential in the wood;
From this live encounter came the work
Which you ascribe to the spirits.'

Chuang Tzu

Ten Commandments for Reducing Stress

1. Thou shalt not be perfect, nor even try.
2. Thou shalt not try to be all things to all people.
3. Thou shalt not leave things undone that ought to be done.
4. Thou shalt not spread thyself too thin.
5. Thou shalt learn to say no.
6. Thou shalt schedule time for thyself, and thy supportive network.
7. Thou shalt switch off and do nothing – regularly.
8. Thou shalt be boring, inelegant, untidy and unattractive at times.
9. Thou shalt not feel guilty.
10. Thou shalt not be thy own worst enemy, but be thy best friend.

Author unknown

Our Deepest Fear

Our deepest fear is not that we are inadequate. Our deepest fear is that we are powerful beyond measure. It is our light, not our darkness, that most frightens us. We ask ourselves, who am I to be brilliant, gorgeous, talented, and fabulous? Actually, who are you not to be? You are a child of God.

Your playing small doesn't serve the world. There's nothing enlightened about shrinking so that other people won't feel insecure around you. We are all meant to shine, as children do. We are born to make manifest the glory of God that is within us. It's not just in some of us, it's in everyone.

And as we let our own light shine, we unconsciously give other people permission to do the same. As we are liberated from our own fear, our presence automatically liberates others.

Nelson Mandela

God Counts on Us

Only God can create
But we are called upon to value that creation.
Only God can give life
But we are called to transmit it and respect it.
Only God can make growth happen
But we are called to guide it and give it direction.
Only God can give faith
But we are called to be signs of God for one another.
Only God can give love
But we are called to grow in caring for each other.
Only God can give hope
But we are called to enable people to believe in themselves.
Only God can give power and energy
But we are called upon to get things going.
Only God can give peace
But we are called to build bonds that bring people together.
Only God can give happiness
But we are invited to laugh.
Only God is the way
But we are called to show it to others.
Only God is the light
But we are called to let it shine forth in the world.
Only God can make miracles happen
But we are invited to offer our five loaves and two fishes.
Only God can do the impossible
But it is up to us to do what is possible.

Author unknown

Tomorrow

Tomorrow is a dream that leads me onward.
Tomorrow is a path I've yet to choose,
A chance I've yet to take,
A friend I've yet to make.
It's all the talent I've yet to use.
Tomorrow is a dream that leads me onward,
Always just a step ahead of me.
It's the joy I've yet to know,
The love I've yet to show.
For it's the person I've yet to be.

Karen Ravn

Eyes to See

It is through the power of imagination that we can see beyond the visible world and realise that there is more to life than that which meets the empirical eye. The eye of the imagination is the lamp that lights up what is lacking in life and enables us to see the world as suggestive of something more than that which appears at first glance. Imagination enables us to re-order the world … to open up an alternative world by invoking images, employing metaphors and weaving narratives which lift us out of the mundane and the purely prosaic.

Dermot A. Lane

Blessing

May we live so that awe may awaken in us
as we embrace the relationship that is ours with every creature.
May reverence for each difference fill our lives,
may desire for communication motivate our living,
and may we give birth to our creativity
that justice may flourish for all creation in our time.

Amen.

Author unknown

Half-hearted

I wonder if many people feel as I do – that in the society we have created it is very difficult to give your full, sustained attention to anything or anybody for long, that we are compelled to half-do a lot of things, to half-live our lives, half-dream our dreams, half-love our loves? We have made ourselves into half-people. Half-heartedness is a slow, banal killer. It is also, paradoxically, a creepy pathway towards 'success', especially if the half-heartedness is of the polished variety. I think it was D.H. Lawrence who said that the real tragedy of modern man is the loss of heart. I don't think so. I believe our tragedy is the viability of our half-heartedness, our insured, mortgaged, welfare voyage of non-discovery, the committed, corrosive involvement with forces, created by ourselves, that ensure our lives will be half-lived. There's a sad refusal here. A rejection of the unique, fragile gift.

Have we refused some love-offering we should have accepted? Have we organised and unionised ourselves into semi-paralytics?

Brendan Kennelly

Can You Really Say This Creed?

I believe in God the Father of all peoples, who has given us the earth for our possession.

I believe in the spirit of God, the source of strength that energises the world and works in all men of good will.

I do not believe that might gives right, nor in the language of guns, nor the power of the wealthy.

I wish to believe in the right of the oppressed, openness to peace and the power of the poor.

I wish to believe that all women and men are equal. I do not believe in bigotry and racism.

I do not believe that I can protest against injustice in Asia or Africa, if I tolerate injustice in my own country.

I wish to believe that rights must exist everywhere, and that I am not free while there exists one single enslaved person.

I do not believe that war and hunger are inevitable.

I wish to believe that the whole world is my home, that the worst violence is to deprive others of life itself by denying them existence, or a home.

I will never believe that the struggles of the oppressed for liberation are useless.

I will never believe that the people's dreams must remain dreams.

I dare to believe in the dream of God himself, a new heaven and a new earth, where there will be justice and equality, where God will be all and in all.

Author unknown

THE STORY OF THE PENCIL

A boy was watching his grandmother write a letter. At one point, he asked: 'Are you writing a story about what we've done? Is it a story about me?' His grandmother stopped writing her letter and said to her grandson: 'I am writing about you, actually, but more important than the words is the pencil I'm using. I hope you will be like this pencil when you grow up.'

Intrigued, the boy looked at the pencil. It didn't seem very special. 'But it's just like any other pencil I've ever seen!'

'That depends on how you look at things. It has five qualities which, if you manage to hang on to them, will make you a person who is always at peace with the world.' First quality: you are capable of great things, but you must never forget that there is a hand guiding your steps. We call that hand God, and he always guides us according to his will.

'Second quality: now and then, I have to stop writing and use a sharpener. That makes the pencil suffer a little, but afterwards, he's much sharper. So you, too, must learn to bear certain pains and sorrows, because they will make you a better person.

'Third quality: the pencil always allows us to use an eraser to rub out any mistakes. This means that correcting something we did is not necessarily a bad thing; it helps to keep us on the road to justice.

'Fourth quality: what really matters in a pencil is not its wooden exterior, but the graphite inside. So always pay attention to what is happening inside you.

'Finally, the pencil's fifth quality: it always leaves a mark. In just the same way, you should know that everything you do in life will leave a mark, so try to be conscious of that and in your everyday action.'

Paulo Coelho

The Perfect Church

If you should find the perfect church
Without one fault or smear,
For goodness' sake, don't join that church.
You'd spoil the atmosphere.

If you should find the perfect church
Where all anxieties cease,
Then pass it by, lest joining it
You spoil the masterpiece.

If you should find the perfect church
Then don't you ever dare
To tread upon holy ground
You'd be a misfit there!

But since no perfect church exists
Made of imperfect men,
Then let's cease looking for that church
And love the church we're in!

Author unknown

Lessons from Nature

There is Religion in Everything Around Us

There is religion in everything around us,
A calm and holy religion
In the unbreathing things of Nature.
It is a meek and blessed influence,
Stealing in as it were unaware upon the heart,
It comes quickly, and without excitement,
It has no terror, no gloom,
It does not rouse up the passions,
It is untrammelled by creeds …
It is written in the arched sky,
It looks out from every star,
It is on the sailing cloud and in the invisible wind,
It is among the hills and valleys of the earth
Where the shrubless mountain-top pierces the thin atmosphere of eternal winter,
Or where the mighty forest fluctuates before the strong wind,
With its dark waves of green foliage,
It is spread out like a legible language upon the broad face of an unsleeping ocean,
It is the poetry of Nature,
It is that which uplifts the spirit within us …
And which opens to our imagination a wonder of spiritual beauty and holiness.

John Ruskin

May Our Eyes Open Amazingly to the Mystery of Summer

May our eyes open amazingly to the mystery of summer.
May our ears open amazingly to the sounds of summer.
May our spines buckle with unknowable beauty.
May the immeasurable touch every fibre of our beings.
May the colour of the countryside blossom in our hearts.
May the music of summer be on our lips.
May the fragrance of primrose, buttercup and daisy encircle us.
May the warmth of the sun relax our muscles, and refresh our minds.
May the whole community of life be truly alive with the energy of summer.

Amen.

Author unknown

Trees

I think that I shall never see
A poem lovely as a tree

A tree whose hungry mouth is pressed
Against the earth's sweet flowing breast;

A tree that looks at God all day,
And lifts her leafy arm to pray;

A tree that may in summer wear
A nest of robins in her hair

Upon whose bosom snow has lain
Who intimately lives with rain.

Poems are made by fools like me,
But only God can make a tree.

Joyce Kilmer

The Robin and the Sparrow

Said the robin to the sparrow,
'I should really like to know,
Why these anxious human beings
Rush about and worry so.'

Said the sparrow to the robin,
'Friend I think that it must be,
That they have no Heavenly Father,
Such as cares for you and me.'

Author unknown

Sunflower Prayer

The sunflower turns and greets the morning sun with the fullness of its face. And as the sun travels across the sky, the sunflower follows … until at sunset, the sunflower lowers its head to await the next dawn.

Lord, help me like the sunflower to keep my focus always on you. Though you shed your blood to cleanse me, I know that each act I do without love or caring robs me of the fullness of what I might have been. You and all the angels and saints in heaven look on as I walk through my life, sometimes drawing closer, sometimes falling back. I know that it is neither you or the evil one that takes me a step closer or further away. It is my own acts that determine my progress towards eternity with you.

So I pray that you send me the grace and wisdom to be like the sunflower. May I always keep my focus fixed firmly on you!

Amen.

Author unknown

The Seasons in the Heart

There are four seasons within the clay heart. When it is winter in the world of nature, all the colours have vanished; everything is reduced to grey, black or white. All the visions and beautiful rich colouring of nature thin out completely. Grass disappears from the land and the earth itself is frozen and perished in a bleak self-retraction. In wintertime, nature withdraws. A tree loses all its leaves and retires inwards. When it is wintertime in your life, you are going through pain, difficulty or turbulence. It is now wise to follow the instinct of nature and withdraw into yourself. When it is winter in your soul it is unwise to pursue any new endeavours. You have to lie low and shelter until this bleak, emptying time passes on. This is nature's remedy. It minds itself in hibernation. When there is great pain in your life, you, too, need sanctuary in the shelter of your own soul.

One of the beautiful transitions in nature is the transition from winter into springtime. An old Zen mystic said, when the flower blooms it is spring everywhere. When the first innocent, infant-like flower appears on the earth, one senses nature stirring beneath the frozen surface. There is a lovely phrase in Gaelic, '*ag borradh*', meaning that there is a quivering life about to break forth. The wonderful colours and the new life the earth receives makes spring a time of great exuberance and hope. In a certain sense, spring is the youngest season. Winter is the oldest season. Winter was there from the very beginning. It reigned amidst the silence and bleakness of nature for hundreds of millions of years before vegetation. Spring is a youthful season; it comes forth in a rush of life and promise, hope and possibility. At the heart of the spring there is a great inner longing. It is the time when desire and memory stir towards each other. Consequently, springtime in your soul is a wonderful time to undertake some new adventure, some new project, or to make some important decisions in your life. If you undertake this, when it is springtime in your soul, then the rhythm, the energy and the hidden light of your own clay works with you. You are in the flow of your own growth and potential. Springtime in the soul can be beautiful, hopeful and strengthening. You can make difficult transitions very naturally in an unforced and spontaneous way.

Spring blossoms and grows into summertime. In summertime nature is bedecked with colour. There is a great lushness everywhere, a richness and depth of texture. Summertime is a time of light, growth and arrival. You feel that the secret life of the year, hidden in the winter and coming out in the spring, has really blossomed in the summertime.

Thus, when it is summertime in your soul, it is a time of great balance. You are in the flow of your own nature. You can take as many risks as you like, and you will always land on your feet. There is enough shelter and depth of texture around you to completely ground, balance and mind you.

Summertime grows into autumn. Autumn is one of my favourite times of the year; seeds sown in the spring, nurtured by the summer, now yield their fruit in autumn. It is harvest, the homecoming of the seeds' long and lonely journey through darkness and silence under the earth's surface. Harvest is one of the great feasts of the year. It was a very important time in Celtic culture. The fertility of the earth yielded its fruitfulness. Correspondingly, when it is autumn in your life, the things that happened in the past, or the experiences that were sown in the clay of your heart, almost unknown to you, now yield their fruit. Autumntime in a person's life can be a time of great gathering. It is a time for harvesting the fruits of your experiences.

John O'Donohue

The Church Can Learn From Elephants

All organisations, including the Church, can be likened to elephants because both come to see their own worlds through a process of conditioning. Fully grown elephants are conditioned to remain in place because when young they are shackled to stakes deeply rooted in the ground; mature elephants could pull the stakes up, but their conditioning is so strong that they do not attempt to move. As they were trained to act, so they do. Cultures and organisations are like this; once dynamic and mobile like young elephants, they later become conditioned to the status quo. The axiom is 'We have always done it this way, so why change!'

Author unknown

Silly Geese – Or Are They?

By flying in v-formation, as each bird flaps its wings, the whole flock adds 71 per cent more flying range than if each bird flew alone. People who share a common direction and a sense of community can get where they want more quickly and easily because they are travelling on the trust generated by all.

When the lead goose gets tired, it rotates back into the formation so that it can continue to take advantage of the lifting power immediately in front. The geese in formation honk from behind to encourage those up front to keep up their speed. We need to be sure that our honking from behind is encouragement (and not something else).

When a goose gets sick or wounded or shot down, two geese will drop out of formation and follow the one to help and protect. They stay with the other until that one is either able to fly again or dies. If we have as much sense as geese, we will stand by each other in all circumstances.

Lord, you give marvellous, inbred wisdom to your creatures; instil in us the wisdom we need to carry on your work with the love and support from each other that will enable us to succeed.

Author unknown

The Earth

God says
I am the strength of the rock, the iron in our blood.
I am the copper in the watercress,
The calcium in your broccoli,
The magnesium in your carrots.
I am the dance of decaying leaves.
I am the energy that produces the oak.
I am the power behind the transformation of seeds.
I am the hidden food of flowers, of plants, of trees.
I am the worm aerating your soil.
I am the activity of the microbe.
I am the miracle of all growing things.
I am the ice age splitting the rock.
I am the cradle of the primrose.
I am the source of all food.
I am the health of wholesome food.
I am the bond of shared food.
I am who I am in soil.

Author unknown

Deep Peace

Deep peace of the Running Wave to you.
Deep peace of the Flowing Air to you.
Deep peace of the Quiet Earth to you.
Deep peace of the Shining Stars to you.
Deep peace of the Son of Peace to you.

A Gaelic blessing

Prayer Before an Empty Tree

Jesus,
You move through each season with your magic wand
One by one you have taken my leaves from me
I am the story of your emptiness
You have told me well.

The part of me that feels stripped cries out to you
'How can I give shade with so much gone?'

Again I feel your magic wand
You speak to me of an inner shade whose name is peace
The gift that comes from letting go.
Your story continues to be told in me.
Your story continues to unfold in me.
And suddenly, when I look again
I realise that what you have taken from me
Has only made me free to see.

I am your story of glory!

Author unknown

Earth's Crammed With Heaven

from 'Aurora Leigh'

Earth's crammed with heaven,
And every common bush afire with God:
But only he who sees, takes off his shoes,
The rest sit round it, and pluck blackberries.

Elizabeth Barrett Browning

The Easter Challenge

You believe because you can see . . .
Happy are those who have not seen and yet believe.
John 20:29

Every year it happens:
earth shakes her sleepy head,
still a bit wintered and dull,
and feels new life stirring.

Every year cocoons give up their treasures,
fresh shoots push through brown leaves,
seemingly dead branches shine with green,
and singing birds find their way home.

Every year we hear the stories
empty tomb, surprise grievers,
runners with news and revelation,
unexpected encounters,
conversations on the road,
tales of nets filling with fish,
and breakfast on a seashore.

And every year
the dull and dead in us
meets our Easter challenge:
to be open to the unexpected,
to believe beyond our security,
to welcome God in every form,
and trust in our own greening.

Joyce Rupp

REFLECTION ON THE WORLD

How do you see the world? Is it full of ugliness or is it full of beauty?

A stunningly beautiful sunset was pointed out to a troubled young man some years ago, and his response was, 'If you've seen one sunset, you've seen 'em all.' It was a remarkable statement, not just in its utter falseness, but in that it revealed how cut off from the outer world this young person was. He was incapable of walking in beauty. It surrounded him, but he could not see it.

How like this young man are we though? How well do we experience the beauty around us? As we rush from one obligation to another, do we attend to the beauty of our world? What would it be like to walk in beauty all the time? What would be required of us?

When we walk in beauty we are connected. The universe walks with us. We are in our place and we are aware of the beauty around us. Our eye may be caught by the colourful flower, but we must direct our attention to it to recognise its beauty. So there is an exchange between the beautiful and the witness to the beauty. It is said, 'Beauty is in the eye of the beholder.' We must be awake to recognise beauty. We must have our eyes open to the world to see its beauty.

Recognition of beauty is an act of love. When our hearts are open to love, the world is more beautiful. When we are overcome by hate, all we see is ugliness. When the world looks beautiful to us, it is a sign that we are in a harmonious situation with the universe. Let us prepare ourselves to walk in beauty.

Author unknown

Knowing and Celebrating God

Celebrating the God of Life

We believe in the God of life
who did not create death.
We are followers of a God
who loves and defends life;
who gives over his life to all
to show us love;
a God who endures suffering and death,
a God who is risen,
the Way, the Truth and the Life;
a God who still invites us
to overcome all that is evil,
all that brings pain, suffering and injustice,
and to celebrate the life
that God desires, in abundance,
for us all.

Extract from Order of Service, Christian Aid Week, 1996

The Merton Prayer

Lord, I have no idea where I'm going.
I do not see the road ahead of me.
I cannot know for certain where it will really end.
Nor do I really know myself.
And the fact that I think I am doing your will,
Does not mean that I am actually doing it.
But I believe that the desire to please you,
Does in fact please you,
And I hope that I have this desire.
I know that if I do this,
You will lead me by the right road,
Though I may know nothing about it.
Therefore I trust you always.
Though I may seem to be lost
And in the shadow of death,
I will not fear, for you are with me,
And you will never leave me to face my perils alone.

Thomas Merton

This Jesus Challenges Me

I am FURIOUS, and he tells me: FORGIVE!
I am AFRAID, and he tells me: TAKE COURAGE!
I have DOUBTS, and he says to me: HAVE CONFIDENCE!
I feel RESTLESS, and he says to me: BE CALM!

I prefer to go MY OWN WAY, and he tells me: COME AND FOLLOW ME!
I make MY OWN PLANS, and he says to me: FORGET ABOUT THEM!
I aim towards MATERIAL GOODS, and he says: LEAVE THEM BEHIND!
I want SECURITY, and he says: I PROMISE YOU ABSOLUTELY NOTHING!

I like to live MY OWN LIFE and he says: LOSE YOUR LIFE!
I believe I AM GOOD, and he tells me: GOOD IS NOT ENOUGH!
I like to BE THE BOSS, and he says: SERVE!
I like to COMMAND OTHERS, and says: OBEY!

I like to UNDERSTAND, and he says: BELIEVE!
I like CLARITY, and he speaks to me in PARABLES!
I like POETRY, and he speaks to me in REALITIES!
I like my TRANQUILITY, and he likes me to be DISTURBED!

I like VIOLENCE, and he says: PEACE BE WITH YOU!
I draw the SWORD, and he says: PUT THAT AWAY!
I think of REVENGE, and he says: OFFER THE OTHER CHEEK!
I choose HATRED, and he says: LOVE YOUR ENEMIES!

I try to sow HARMONY, and he says: I HAVE COME TO CAST FIRE UPON THE EARTH!
I like to be the GREATEST, and he says: I LEARN TO BE AS SMALL AS A CHILD!
I like to remain HIDDEN, and he says: LET YOUR LIGHT SHINE!
I look at the BEST PLACE, and he says: SIT IN THE LAST BENCH!
I like to be NOTICED, and he says: PRAY IN YOUR ROOM BEHIND LOCKED DOORS!

No, I don't understand this Jesus. He provokes me. He confuses me. Like so many of his disciples, I too, would like to follow another master who would be more certain and less demanding. But I experience almost the same as Peter: 'I do not know of anyone else, WHO HAS THE WORDS OF ETERNAL LOVE!'

Author unknown

The Fool

Since the wise men have not spoken, I speak that am only a fool;
A fool that hath loved his folly,
Yea, more than the wise men their books or their counting houses or their quiet homes,
Or their fame in men's mouths;
A fool that in all his days hath done never a prudent thing,
Never hath counted the cost, nor recked if another reaped
The fruit of his mighty sowing, content to scatter the seed;
A fool that is unrepentant, and that soon at the end of all
Shall laugh in his lonely heart as the ripe ears fall to the reaping-hooks
And the poor are filled that were empty,
Tho' he go hungry.

I have squandered the splendid years that the Lord God gave to my youth
In attempting impossible things, deeming them alone worth the toil.
Was it folly or grace? Not men shall judge me, but God.
I have squandered the splendid years:
Lord, if I had the years I would squander them over again,
Aye, fling them from me!
For this I have heard in my heart, that a man shall scatter, not hoard,
Shall do the deed of today, nor take thought of tomorrow's teen,
Shall not bargain or huxter with God; or was it a jest of Christ's
And is this my sin before men, to have taken Him at His word?
The lawyers have sat in council, the men with the keen, long faces,
And said, 'This man is a fool,' and others have said, 'He blasphemeth';
And the wise have pitied the fool that hath striven to give a life
In the world of time and space among the bulks of actual things,
To a dream that was dreamed in the heart, and that only the heart could hold.

O wise men, riddle me this: what if the dream come true?
What if the dream come true? and if millions unborn shall dwell
In the house that I shaped in my heart, the noble house of my thought?
Lord, I have staked my soul, I have staked the lives of my kin
On the truth of Thy dreadful word. Do not remember my failures,
But remember this my faith
And so I speak.

Yea, ere my hot youth pass, I speak to my people and say:
Ye shall be foolish as I; ye shall scatter, not save;
Ye shall venture your all, lest ye lose what is more than all;
Ye shall call for a miracle, taking Christ at His word.
And for this I will answer, O people, answer here and hereafter,
O people that I have loved, shall we not answer together?

Pádraig Pearse

Weaver God

We come to you,
or – more the truth – you find us,
disconnected and out of sorts.
We are disheartened by our failures,
discouraged by our weakness,
and little that we do seems worthy of your grace.
Restore our fortunes. Restore our future.
Weave for us the tapestry
on which our lives are stretched.
Give us patience
with the endless back and forth
of shuttle, hand and effort.
We look too closely
seeing only strands and knots
and snarled threads of too much trying
or not at all.
Grant us eyes to see the whole of which we are a part.
In the end, we ask for gentleness with ourselves,
acceptance of our less than perfect ways.
We pray that what we do and what you weave
form patterns clear to all,
of mercy in the warp of it
and love throughout.

Prayer:
We ask your blessing, weaver God.
We need your steadfast presence.
In our discouragement and fatigue,
grant us laughter and support.
In our vision, give us zeal.
In our weakness, we ask that you accept us,
and in the beauty that is ours
grant that we might stand in truth.

Bless us now, in all things good and human.
For things woven and still to be,
We pray in thanks. Amen.

Author unknown

The Burning Bush Prayer

Creator of fire and water,
Your burning bush has turned
    into a bubbling brook
And I have taken off my shoes
    having heard you call my name.

You do not speak in fire only, Lord.
In water you have sung your songs
And you are singing still.
Today you chant a memory-song
    to my grown-up heart.

You are washing my anxiety away.
You are reminding me of days of old
    when I had time to play.
I stand barefoot upon the stones,
    the rushing water and lapping at my heels.
The sharp stones pierce my grown-up soles.
My tough child-feet have worn away
    as I grew up, forgetting to play.

Creator of the rocks and streams,
I'm growing up once more
I'm taking off my shoes
    and remembering to adore.

My feet are getting tough again,
    my heart is getting young.

Author unknown

A Precious Place of Peace

Sooner or later you are bound to become terribly rattled, upset, disappointed, annoyed or confused. Yet down in the depths of your soul, a tiny pocket of peace remains, a small cleft in the rocks where there is calm, no matter how bad the day becomes. Even when you momentarily lose track of this deep, inner stronghold, it usually resurfaces fairly soon. I'm not speaking about a fleeting emotion like happiness or even inner joy. I mean a safe harbour from the storms of life, a shelter that allows you to survive …

I have survived the swirling tides of life because I discovered a little harbour inside my soul – a haven that I didn't build, a refuge that I didn't set apart from the winds of life. Sometimes in the midst of storms, I couldn't find this sanctuary, but I knew it was there anyway … The God of peace, our Father, provides this inner haven for each of us, a shelter that allows us to survive during difficult times, a place where we can receive the light of grace. If we are trying desperately to hold onto him, God will allow us to find this precious place of peace.

Fr Benedict J. Groeschel, CFR

Pilgrimage Prayer

Life-giving God, we thank you.
You have always watched over our journeyings.
You have blessed us with the signs of your presence.
We come to you now as we find ourselves
needing to take up the staff of pilgrimage once more.
We are in need of energy and renewed hope.
We are in need of your grace
to unsettle and re-direct our hearts.

You call us to announce your love and your vision,
to take a prophetic stance for justice and peace,
for the poor, the powerless and the lowly ones.
Now we proclaim the sacredness of each person.
May we be Good News
as we minister and are ministered to.
Lord, may our pilgrimage together
be an opportunity to give thanks,
to redefine our vision,
to search, and to be shaped and reshaped
through reflection, interaction, challenge
and your forming love.
May we find among us the light of tomorrow's dreaming.

Creating God, may we go forward,
ever mindful of your truth
which leads and guides us.
We pray this through Jesus our brother.
Amen.

Author unknown

Prayer to the God of Mystery and Struggle

To the God of Mystery,
whom I see dimly in flickering stars,
whose heartbeat I hear in the roaring seas,
whose presence I sense in the spring and winter air,
you are behind all, you support all,
we have belief, help our unbelief.

To the God of justice and fairness,
our loving Father who watches over us,
whose challenge I feel in the choices I make,
who reminds me to love when I feel drawn to hate,
who teaches me the way that will lead to life,
help me to have no fear but to know that you loved us first.

To the God of care and compassion,
who holds each one of us close like a mother, a child,
whose hand I hold each step of the way,
to whom I unburden myself in times of stress,
who is always there in each passing second,
come closer still; make your home in me.

To the God of struggle,
who holds the poor and broken ones dear,
who sets prisoners free and gives sight to the blind,
who is still creating this world in your image and likeness,
work with us and give us strength to work with you,
until all our brothers and sisters live in freedom and dignity.

Amen.

Author unknown

Take, Bless, Break and Give

In the Eucharist, bread is taken, blessed, broken and given.
In life we are taken, blessed, broken and given.
The priest takes the bread in his hands and blesses it during the eucharistic prayer;
then he breaks it and it is given to us as the Body of Christ.
Through our birth and baptism we are taken into God's hands;
as the bread is taken, so too are we.
In life we are blessed by family, friends, love and joy;
as the bread is blessed so too are we.
We are broken by failure, sin, pain and heartbreak;
as the bread is broken, so too are we.
In death we are given back to the mystery from which we came;
as the bread is given, so too are we.
When we take, bless, break and give bread to one another,
we believe the Lord to be especially present in our midst.
But we must learn to accept that, in his memory,
we will be taken, blessed, broken and given
for the life of the world.

Michael Drumm and Tom Gunning

from St Patrick's Breastplate

Christ be with me, Christ be within me,
Christ be behind me, Christ be before me,
Christ beside me, Christ to win me,
Christ to comfort and restore me,
Christ beneath me, Christ above me,
Christ in quiet, Christ in danger,
Christ in the hearts of all that love me,
Christ in the mouth of friend and stranger …

An Irish Blessing

May the blessing of light be upon you,
light on the outside, light on the inside.
With God's sunlight shining on you,
may your heart glow with warmth, like a turf fire
that welcomes friends and strangers alike.

May the light of the Lord shine from your eyes,
like a candle in the window,
welcoming the weary traveller.

May the blessing of God's soft rain be on you,
falling gently on your head,
refreshing your soul with the sweetness
of little flowers newly blooming.

May the strength of the winds of heaven bless you,
carrying the rain to wash your spirit clean,
sparkling after in the sunlight.

May the blessing of God's earth be with you,
and as you walk the roads, may you always
have a kind word for those you meet.

May you understand the strength and
power of God in a thunderstorm in winter,
and the quiet beauty of creation,
and the calm of a summer sunset.

And may you come to realise that insignificant as you may seem
in this great universe you are an important part of God's plan.
May he watch over you, and keep you safe from harm.

Author unknown

The Celestial Surgeon

If I have faltered more or less
In my great task of happiness;
If I have moved among my race
And shown no glorious morning face;
If beams from happy human eyes
Have moved me not; if morning skies,
Books and my food; and summer rain
Knocked on my sullen heart in vain:
Lord, Thy most pointed pleasure take
And stab my spirit broad awake;
Or, Lord, if too obdurate I,
Choose Thou, before that spirit die,
A piercing pain, a killing sin,
And to my dead heart run them in!

Robert Louis Stevenson

INTERVIEW WITH GOD

'Come in,' God said. 'So you would like to interview me?'

'If you have the time,' I said.

God smiled and said, 'My time is eternity and is enough to do everything. What question do you have in mind to ask me?'

'What surprises you most about mankind?'

God answered: 'That they get bored of being children, are in a rush to grow up, and then long to be children again. That they lose their health to make money and then lose their money to restore their health.

'That by thinking anxiously about the future, they forget the present, such that they live neither for the present nor the future.

'That they live as if they will never die, and they die as if they have never lived ...'

God's hands took mine and we were silent for a while and then I asked: 'As a parent, what are some of life's lessons you want your children to learn?'

God replied with a smile: 'To learn that they cannot make anyone love them. What they can do is to let themselves be loved.

'To learn that what is most valuable is not what they have in their lives, but who they have in their lives.

'To learn that it is not good to compare themselves to others. All will be judged individually on their own merits, not as a group on a comparison basis!

'To learn that a rich person is not the one who has the most, but is one who needs the least.

'To learn that it only takes a few seconds to open profound wounds in persons we love, and that it takes many years to heal them.

'To learn to forgive by practicing forgiveness.

'To learn that there are persons that love them dearly, but simply do not know how to express or show their feelings.

'To learn that money can buy everything but happiness.

'To learn that two people can look at the same thing and see it totally differently.

'To learn that a true friend is someone who knows everything about them and likes them anyway.

'To learn that it is not always enough that they be forgiven by others, but that they have to forgive themselves.'

I sat there for a while, enjoying the moment. I thanked him for his time and for all that he has done for me and my family, and he replied: 'Any time. I'm here twenty-four hours a day. All you have to do is ask for me, and I'll answer.'

People will forget what you said. People will forget what you did, but people will never forget how you made them feel.

Author unknown

God on Call

Our God's on call
    Hours around the clock
Offices everywhere
    Our God on demand

No period waiting
    Parental consent waived
Few questions asked
    Our God on demand

No appointment needed
    Just walk right in
No paper trail here
    Our God on demand

It's legal in my state
    Minor that I am
I'm old enough for seeking
    Our God on demand

There's little politicking
    No placards to be seen
I'm among the silent number
    Seeking God on demand

Our God's on call
    Hours around the clock
Offices everywhere
    Our God on demand

Barbara Bradley

The Difference

I got up early one morning
and rushed right into the day.
I had so much to accomplish
that I didn't have time to pray.

Problems just tumbled about me,
and grew heavier with each task.
'Why doesn't God help me?' I wondered.
He answered, 'You didn't ask.'

I wanted to see joy and beauty,
but the day toiled on, grey and bleak.
I wondered why God didn't show me,
He said, 'But you didn't seek.'

I tried to come into God's presence;
I used all my keys at the lock.
God gently and lovingly chided,
'My child, you didn't knock.'

I woke up early this morning,
and paused before entering the day.
I had so much to accomplish
that I had to take time to pray.

Grace L. Naessens

The Soldier's Prayer

Look God: I have never spoken to you,
But now, I want to say, 'How do you do?'
You see God, they told me you did not exist,
And like a fool, I believed all of this.

Last night from a shell hole I saw your sky;
I figured right then they had told me a lie.
Had I taken the time to see the things you made,
I would know they weren't calling a spade a spade.

I wonder, God, if you would shake my hand?
Somehow, I feel you'd understand.
It's strange I had to come to this horrible place,
Before I had time to see your face.

Well, there isn't much more to say,
But I sure am glad, God, I met you today.
The zero hour will soon be here,
But I am not afraid since I know you're near.

The signal! Well, God, I'll have to go.
I like you a lot, this I want you to know.
Look now, this will soon be a horrible fight.
Who knows? I may even come to your house tonight!

Though I wasn't friendly with you before,
I wonder, God, if you'd wait at the door?

Look I am crying, me shedding tears!
I wish I had known you these many years.

Well, I will have to go now, God, goodbye.
Strange, since I met you, I am not afraid to die.

Author unknown

God's Spirit

May God's Spirit of Life be with us, life to be cherished and nurtured and lived to its fullness.

May God's Spirit of Wisdom be with us, guiding us to seek always with the eyes of faith and truth.

May God's Creative Spirit be with us, inspiring us to respond creatively to what is new and life-giving.

May God's Spirit of Peace be with us, guiding us always towards the way of peace.

May God's Spirit surround us with Light.
May God's Spirit open us to the mystery of today.

Amen.

Author unknown

Circle Us, O God

Circle me, O God, let Your arms enfold me,
Circle me, O God, let Your love surround me.
Circle me, O God, let Your light shine brightly,
Circle me, Circle me, O God.

Circle me, O God, when I'm tired and weary,
Circle me, O God, when despair is near.
Circle me, O God, let Your peace surround me,
Circle me, Circle me, O God.

Circle me, O God, when I'm weak and restless,
Circle me, O God, be my hope, my strength.
Circle me, O God, let Your presence guide me,
Circle me, Circle me, O God.

Author unknown

Prayer for God's Blessing

1. May the God of strength be with us, holding us in strong-fingered hands and may we be the sacrament of his strength to those whose hands we hold.

May the blessing of strength be on us.

2. May the God of gentleness be with us, caressing us with sunlight and rain; may his tenderness shine through us to warm all who are hurt or lonely.

May the blessing of gentleness be on us.

3. May the God of mercy be with us, forgiving us, beckoning us, encouraging us; may our readiness to forgive calm the fears and deepen the trust of those who have hurt us.

May the blessing of mercy be on us.

4. May the God of wonder be with us, delighting us, enchanting our senses, filling our hearts, giving us wide-open eyes for seeing the splendour in the humble and majestic and may we open the eyes and hearts of the blind, the deaf and the cynical.

May the blessing of wonder be on us.

5. May the God of compassion be with us, holding us close when we are weary and hurt and alone, and when there is rain in our hearts. May we be the warm eyes of compassion for all those who reach out to us in need.

May the blessing of compassion be on us.

6. May the God of peace be with us, stilling the heart that hammers with fear or doubt or confusion; and may the warm mantle of our peace cover those who are troubled or anxious.

May the blessing of peace be on us.

7. May the God of love be with us, listening to us, telling us his secrets, giving himself to us. May his love in us light fires of faith and hope and may the fires grow and burn and inflame the earth. May his love glow in our eyes and meet his love glowing in the eyes of our brothers and sisters.

May the blessing of love be on us.

8. May the Triune God be within all of us, Father, Son and Spirit. Drawing us ever nearer, speaking to us of sisterhood and brotherhood where distinction of persons is also oneness of being. May the blessings of community arise from within us, radiate around us and remain for ever.

May the blessing of community be on us.

Lord, produce in us a harvest of the Spirit: love for you, for one another; joy in all that you do for us; peace because you have forgiven our sins; patience in suffering; kindness, especially to those who are less than kind to us; goodness that is genuine; faithfulness in all that we undertake.

Author unknown

An Anointing Psalm

Anoint me with the oil of integrity, O God, and the seal of your sanctifying Spirit.
Anoint my head so that all my thoughts come from the well of your being, to fill me with grace and peace.
Anoint my eyes so that I might see your presence and providence clearly.

Anoint my ears that I might hear the cry of the poor all around me and whisper your word.
Anoint my lips that I might proclaim the Good News of your mission and the meaning of Jesus Christ.
Anoint my hands to hold and heal the many lives that are broken that I may do good, do what I must to bring hope into hopelessness.

Anoint my feet to walk in your ways, to run and never grow weary, to stand up for justice unafraid.
Anoint my heart with warmth and compassion and a genuine generosity toward all who are in need.
Anoint my spirit for mission, that I might have the courage to respond with the whole of my being to the daily demands of grace.

I believe in God whose will is wholeness:
I believe in Christ who will guide me on my journey:
I believe in the Holy Spirit who gives each of us the power to do more than we can believe or dare to ask for.
Believing all this, engaging with challenge, I step across the edge of time through the door into the future of my journey to wholeness in Christ.

Amen.

Author unknown

Meeting God

Meeting God can be very simple. If it is not simple, and no voice speaks in our silence, then we should consider the following:

Perhaps God cannot be God to us, because we are not ourselves, our true selves to God. We have not prayed as we are, but as we thought we ought to be, or as others want us to be, or as we think God thinks we ought to be. This last can verge on blasphemy.

Perhaps we fail to recognise God in a chance remark we overhear, in a stray thought passing through our mind, or in a phrase from a prayer book that resonates with us.

Perhaps we do not like what God says, but are frightened to say so and pretend we never met God. This avoidance is natural because in the sight of God our success can be failure, and our ambitions mere dust.

Perhaps we are satisfied with our lives and do not really want to meet God. So we chant our prayers and sing our hymns to prevent a few moments' silence, for God speaks in silence.

Perhaps we have not allowed God to judge us because we have already judged ourselves. God knows us better than we know ourselves, loves us more than we think, and may still surprise us.

Perhaps we are frightened about where God is leading us. Is it into a wilderness? Are we being asked to find our security in trusting him? Will we be given the courage equal to his ongoing call?

Meeting God can be simple.

But nothing can happen if we do not will it. If we seek we will find. God will allow us to find him if we seek with trusting hearts through the ever-changing events of our lives.

Author unknown

When I First Saw God

At first, I saw God as my observer, my judge, keeping track of the things I did wrong, so as to know whether I merited heaven or hell when I die. He was there sort of like a magistrate.

I recognised his picture when I saw it, but I really didn't know him. But later on when I met Christ, it seemed as though life was rather like a bike ride, but it was a tandem bike, and I noticed that Christ was in the back helping me pedal. I don't know just when it was that he suggested we change places, but life has not been the same since, apostolic life, that is – Christ makes life exciting.

When I had control, I knew the way. It was rather boring, but predictable ... It was the shortest distance between two points. But when he took the lead, he knew delightfully long cuts, up mountains, and through rocky places at breakneck speeds – it was all I could do to hang on!

Even though it looked like madness, he said 'Pedal!' I worried and was anxious and asked 'Where are you taking me?' He laughed, but no answer, and I started to learn to trust. I forgot my boring life and entered into the adventure. And when I'd say, 'I'm scared,' he'd lean back and touch my hand.

He took me to people that had gifts that I needed. Gifts of healing, acceptance, love, and joy. So many priceless gifts to take on the journey – our journey, my Lord's and mine. Then we were off again. He said, 'Give the gifts away – they're extra baggage, too much weight.' So I did, to the people we met, and found that in giving I received, and my burden was light.

I didn't trust him at first – in control of my life. I thought he'd wreck it. But I discovered he knows bike secrets, knows how to make it bend to take sharp corners; jump to clear high rocks; fly to shorten passages. And I am learning to shut up and pedal in the strangest places, and I'm beginning to enjoy the view and the cool breeze on my face with my delightful constant companion, Christ.

And when I'm sure I just can't do anymore, he just smiles and says ... 'Pedal.'

Author unknown

Advent and Christmas

We Advent Each Other

We Advent each other in simple steps:
Smiles, caring inclusion, polite gestures
Of referent affirmation,
Silently and subtly pointing our way to Bethlehem.
Each journey is singular,
A personal mystery, sojourns of paradox waiting
Yet searching.
We pack our bags differently these days.
The travelling itself may seem burden and
Baggage enough.

The empty crib stands before us.
Hidden at some distant place (always in disguise)
Patiently awaiting our arrival.
The Saviour within us, and about us
Cries out for incarnated birth
Once more to be heart
In a land of hopeless hearts.
The desolate winter of our disbelief can be renewed
In a manger warm with embrace.
So we follow each other's stars,
Whether bright or dim,
Through dark days this December.
Until suddenly home
Where the angels of our gladness shepherd us gently in
Christmas transforms us newborn
Yet again!

Sr Susan Spadinger

'GO AND SEARCH DILIGENTLY FOR THE YOUNG CHILD'

Isn't it strange that it should be the arch-tyrant King Herod who gave what is perhaps the best advice anyone could give at this time of year? That it should be he, the brutal murderer of the babes of Bethlehem, who spoke those words to the Magi, words which inspire us today as much as they encouraged them, 'Go and search diligently for the young child.' (Mt 2:8).

God is full of surprises. We do not always find him where we expect him to be, and then suddenly there comes a hint, a nudge, a throwaway word or a piece of advice from Herod, and there he is. Of all the characters in the Christmas story – Mary, Joseph, the shepherds, the angels, the Magi – Herod is not the one we'd single out as having anything to say to us. But there it is, 'Go and search diligently for the child.'

The wise men took the advice and followed the directions given by Herod. They found the One they were looking for in the place Herod sent them. It was the end of a long search. It was also the beginning of another journey. They were warned in a dream not to return to Herod and they went back by 'another way'. When we meet Jesus, the direction of our life is changed.

So, go down the road of your own heart and look for him there. Speak to him in your own heart and quietly become aware of how loved you are. Search for him in your own heart, yes, but not only there. You do not have to go to Bethlehem today to bring your gifts to the child. Bring them to the forgotten widower, the deserted wife, the neglected neighbour, the backward child, and you bring them to him.

The child is also searching for you. He will never give up this search. 'Behold, I stand at the door and knock' (Rev 3:21). It is not a stranger who stands waiting for you to open the door. He is the one who understands you, does not judge you, does not condemn you, however much you have strayed from the path of truth.

Let us take Herod's advice this Christmas. Let us search diligently for Jesus. Search for him beyond all the hectic preparations, the shopping, the parties, the feasting and the fun. Let us look for the child with all our hearts. We can be sure that, like the Magi, we will find him 'with Mary his mother'.

Author unknown

Seven Gifts That You Can Give

The wise men brought gifts of gold, frankincense and myrrh, but you can do even better. The gifts that Jesus would love to receive from you this Christmas are:

1. Your heart as a place in which to dwell, and as a temple to flood with his love.
2. Your mind for him to fill with noble and positive thoughts.
3. Your dreams and ambitions so that he can fill them with his vision for the world.
4. Your voice so that he can use it to speak words of love, and to share with others how their lives too can be filled with joy.
5. Your hands to reach out to others with his love, and to work to make this world a better place.
6. Your feet to bring the Good News wherever you go.
7. Your suffering, so that he can unite it with his own, and release countless blessings into the world.

Author unknown

Searching in the Wrong Places

When Jesus was born in the stable in Bethlehem, he was the Son of God made human. He was the promised Messiah, the one for whom they had been waiting for years. Yet when he came, very few recognised him; they were not looking for a baby born in a manger. They were looking for someone rich, famous and powerful – a great king or leader. And so they searched in all the wrong places.

So it is often with us also. When we try to find Christ in our world, we look in all the wrong places.
Where do you look when you want to find Christ in your world?
What will you have to say to him when you find him?
What do you think he will have to say to you?

When does the work of Christmas begin? When the star in the sky is gone, when the kings and princes are home, when the shepherds are back with their flocks, the work of Christmas begins – to heal the broken hearted, to feed the hungry, to release the prisoner and bring peace among people.

Author unknown

Christmas

Stable of Bethlehem,
space of tenderness, home of hospitality
to an anxious couple, in search of shelter,
to a newborn child, fragile and vulnerable,
to poor shepherds, on the margins of town and society,
to searching Magi, believing in the promise of the star.

As we rejoice in God with us,
may we become Bethlehem spaces,
open to receive and to embrace
the fragile, the vulnerable, the displaced
in ourselves,
in one another,
in our world.
Christmas,
stillness of God, whisper of love,
breath of God, quiet mystery,
light of joy, holy wisdom,
shadow of God, birth of mercy.

May God be with us in tenderness and love this Christmas.

'For unto us a child is born,
unto us a Son is given.' (Is 9:6)

Author unknown

Homecoming Prayer

'Make your home in me as I make mine in you' – ST JOHN

We invite you into the experience of returning home to God this Christmas, to allow the Word to become flesh again in your life, to make your home in him.

God of welcome and acceptance,
Call me home from the four winds of distraction,
Call me home to my own heart,
Welcome me into your peace.

Call me home from a far country,
Call me home from darkness and sin,
Welcome me into your forgiveness.

Call me home from my place of exile,
Call me home from the Christmas rush,
Help me to make my home with you.

Call me home to my faith and to my church,
Call me home to Bethlehem, to rebirth,
Help me to see divinity in a stable.

Give me a heart for the homeless, for the refugee.
Give me a prayer of healing for homes where
there is violence, grief or separation.
Give me a heart of love for those who are afraid
to come home.
Help us all to turn our houses into homes, into places of
welcome and acceptance for God and one another.

Amen.

Liam Ryan OSA

Seekers of Hope

It's the whole world
that comes with the wise men to the crib,
drawing close to the infant God,
that they might find in him
meaning in life and light for living.

We draw close, Lord,
with all those who have lost hope,
all those for whom faith is nothing more
than a long night to be got through,
all those who have lost the taste
for seeking and struggling …

We draw close, Lord,
with all those who are handicapped in body or mind,
with those who are paralysed in their suffering,
with those left to their loneliness,
whom nobody ever comes to console …

We draw close, Lord,
with all those who've had their place taken,
with those living in poverty and hunger,
with those whose dignity has been trodden on,
with those who have forgotten the colours of peace …

We draw close with confidence
to you, child of the crib.
Look: we've come seeking hope!

Author unknown

A Christmas Prayer

Loving Father, help us to remember the birth
of Jesus, that we may share in the song of the angels,
the gladness of the shepherds,
and the worship of the wise men.
Close the door of hate and
open the door of love all over the world.
Let kindness come with every gift and
good desires with every greeting.
Deliver us from evil by the blessing
which Christ brings, and teach us to
be merry with clean hearts.
May the Christmas morning make us happy
to be thy children, and the Christmas evening
bring us to our beds with grateful thoughts,
forgiving and forgiven, for Jesus' sake.
Amen!

Robert Louis Stevenson

YES VIRGINIA, THERE IS A SANTA CLAUS

We take pleasure in answering thus prominently the communication below, expressing at the same time our great gratification that its faithful author is numbered among the friends of the Sun*:*

Dear Editor, I am eight years old. Some of my little friends say there is no Santa Claus. Papa says, 'If you see it in the *Sun*, it is so.' Please tell me the truth, is there a Santa Claus?

VIRGINIA O'HANLON

Virginia, your little friends are wrong. They have been affected by the scepticism of a sceptical age. They do not believe except they see. They think that nothing can be which is not comprehensible by their little minds. All minds, Virginia, whether they be men's or children's, are little. In this great universe of ours, man is a mere insect, an ant, in his intellect as compared with the boundless world about him, as measured by the intelligence capable of grasping the whole of truth and knowledge.

Yes, Virginia, there is a Santa Claus. He exists as certainly as love and generosity and devotion exist, and you know that they abound and give to your life its highest beauty and joy. Alas! How dreary would be the world if there were no Santa Claus! It would be as dreary as if there were no Virginias. There would be no childlike faith then, no poetry, no romance to make tolerable this existence. We should have no enjoyment, except in sense and sight. The eternal light with which childhood fills the world would be extinguished.

Not believe in Santa Claus! You might as well not believe in fairies. You might get your papa to hire men to watch in all the chimneys on Christmas Eve to catch Santa Claus, but even if you did not see Santa Claus coming down, what would that prove? Nobody sees Santa Claus, but that is no sign that there is no Santa Claus. The most real things in the world are those that neither children nor men can see. Did you ever see fairies dancing on the lawn? Of course not, but that's no proof that they are not there. Nobody can conceive or imagine all the wonders there are unseen and unseeable in the world.

You tear apart the baby's rattle and see what makes the noise inside, but there is a veil covering the unseen world which not the strongest man, nor even the united strength of all the strongest men that ever lived could tear apart. Only faith, poetry, love, romance, can push aside that curtain and view and picture the supernal beauty and glory beyond.

Is it all real? Ah, Virginia, in all this world there is nothing else real and abiding.

No Santa Claus! Thank God! He lives and lives forever. A thousand years from now, Virginia, nay ten times ten thousand years from now, he will continue to make glad the heart of childhood.

FRANCIS P. CHURCH

BACKGROUND TO THE ARTICLE

In 1897, a little New York girl called Virginia O'Hanlon worried about Santa. Some of her school friends claimed there was no Santa and so young Virginia asked her father to tell her the truth.

'It was a habit in our family that whenever any doubts came up as to how to pronounce a word or some question of historical fact was in doubt, we wrote to the Question and Answer column in the *Sun*. Father would always say, "If you see it in the *Sun*, it is so," and that settled the matter,' she was to say years later.

Her letter found its way into the hands of a veteran editor, Francis P. Church. The son a Baptist minister, Church had covered the Civil War for the *New York Times* and had worked on the *New York Sun* for twenty years, more recently as an anonymous editorial writer.

At once, Church knew that there was no avoiding the question. He must answer, and he must answer truthfully. And so he turned to his desk and he began his reply, which was to become one of the most memorable editorials in newspaper history.

Church married shortly after the editorial appeared. He died in April 1906, leaving no children.

Virginia O'Hanlon went on to graduate from Hunter College with a Bachelor of Arts degree at age twenty-one. The following year she received her Master's from Columbia, and in 1912 she began teaching in the New York City school system, later becoming a principal. After forty-seven years, she retired as an educator. Throughout her life she received a steady stream of mail about her Santa Claus letter, and to each reply she attached an attractive printed copy of the Church editorial. Virginia O'Hanlon Douglas died on May 13, 1971, at the age of eighty-one, in a nursing home in Valatie, New York.

Prepare the Way of the Lord

All of us can be like John the Baptist,
preparing the way for Jesus Christ in our families,
among friends, in schools and workplaces,
preparing a space in our hearts for love.

Allow time these days for prayer,
for moments taken in a busy day,
like stopping in the heavy traffic,
and just remembering that Jesus is near.
Take time for friendship, for love, for care,
for those activities that grow our friendship and love
with the people who mean a lot.
Take time these days for the poor,
for ensuring that someone's Christmas
will be better because of your generosity.

Then the songs will be full,
and gifts will be reminders of love,
and Santa, the friend of children,
will be like the Christ-child.

Then love for God and others
will come to birth at Christmas.

Author unknown

Christmas Litany

Let us pray:
Saviour of the world, born in simplicity and joy; cradled in a welcoming manger and nursed by Mary and Joseph, we rejoice with you in your simplicity as we come before you in prayer this Christmas, praying:

Joy of God	be the source of our joy.
Happiness of God	be unity in our families.
Grace of God	be compassion to us sinners.
Calm of God	be our tranquility in times of trouble.
Care of God	be comfort to those who are mentally ill.
Hope of God	be optimism to the down-hearted.
Manger of God	be our Eucharist as we journey through uncertain times.
Way of God	be a sure path for those seeking employment.
Light of God	be hope to those who have lost their financial security.
Image of God	be reflected in our words and in our actions.
Hospitality of God	be our welcome to the rejected and the homeless.
Harmony of God	be our reconciliation and peace.
Integrity of God	be the conscience of each of us and of our leaders.
Justice of God	be our truth and that of our policy makers.
Silence of God	be the tongue of our voiceless and bullied.
Word of God	be Good News to all seekers.
Thanksgiving of God	be our blessing as we journey in renewed faith and trust.
Salvation of God	be our host at the Paschal banquet.

Kathleen M. Murphy

Christmas Prologue

This, tonight,
is the meeting place
of heaven and earth.

For this, tonight,
is the stable
in which God keeps his appointment
to meet his people.

Not many high are here,
not many holy;
not many innocent children,
not many worldly wise;
not all familiar faces,
not all frequent visitors.

But, if tonight
only strangers met,
that would be enough.

For Bethlehem was not the hub of the universe,
nor was the stable a platform for famous folk.

In an out-of-the-way place
which folk never thought to visit –
there God kept and keeps his promise;
there God sends his son.

Wild Goose Worship Group

Christmas Lasts Forever

And now God says to us what he has already said to the world as a whole through his grace-filled birth:

I am there. I am with you. I am your life. I am the gloom in your daily routine. Why will you not bear it? I weep your tears – pour out yours to me, my child. I am your joy. Do not be afraid to be happy, for ever since I wept, joy is the standard of living that is really more suitable than the anxiety and grief of those who think they have no hope. I am the blind alleys of all your paths, for when you no longer know how to go any further, then you have reached me, foolish child, though you are not aware of it. I am in your anxiety, for I have shared it by suffering it. And in doing so, I wasn't even heroic according to the wisdom of the world. I am in the prison of your finiteness, for my love has made me your prisoner. When the totals of your plans and of your life's experiences do not balance out evenly, I am the unresolved remainder. And I know that this remainder, which makes you so frantic, is in reality my love, that you do not understand. I am present in your needs. I have suffered them and now they are transformed but not obliterated from my heart … This reality – incomprehensible wonder of my almighty love – I have sheltered safely in the cold stable of your world. I am there. I no longer go away from this world, even if you do not see me now … I am there. It is Christmas. Light the candles. They have more right to exist than all the darkness. It is Christmas. Christmas lasts forever.

Karl Rahner

Acknowledgements

Dedication page. 'Living Wide Open: Landscapes of the Mind', copyright © 2000 by Dawna Markova, *I Will Not Die an Unlived Life: Reclaiming Purpose and Passion*, Newburyport, MA: Conari Press, 2000.

p. 22. 'Credo' from *All I Really Needed to Know I Learned in Kindergarten*, copyright © 1986, 1988 by Robert L. Fulghum. Used by permission of Villard Books, a division of Random House.

p. 36. 'How to Build a Global Community', Members SWC Community © 1997 www.syracuseculturalworkers.com.

p. 50. 'On Being a Well', Macrina Wiederkehr, *Seasons of Your Heart: Prayers and Reflections, Revised and Expanded*, New York: HarperOne, 1991.

p. 53. 'How Can We?' © Clare McBeath and Tim Presswood, first published in *From Crumbs of Hope: Prayers from the City*, Peterborough, UK: Inspire/MPH, 2006 (available from www.dancingscarecrow.org.uk). Used with kind permission.

p. 57. 'The Good', Brendan Kennelly, *Familiar Strangers: New & Selected Poems 1960–2004*, Northumberland: Bloodaxe Books, 2004.

p. 60. 'The Restless Heart', Ronald Rolheiser, *The Restless Heart: Finding Our Spiritual Home in Times of Loneliness*, New York: Doubleday Religion, 2004.

p. 80. 'Dream Dreams', Debra Hintz, *Prayer Services For Parish Meetings*, Mystic, CT: Twenty-Third Publications, 1983. Reprinted with permission of the author.

p. 89. 'A Blessing of Solitude' and 'A Blessing', and p. 114, 'The Seasons in the Heart', John O'Donohue, *Anam Cara: Spiritual Wisdom From the Celtic World*, London: Bantam Books, 1997.

p. 90. 'Beginners', Denise Levertov. Reprinted by permission of New Directions Publishing Corp. (US, its territories, and Canada) from *Candles in Babylon*, 1982, and Bloodaxe Books (UK) from *New Selected Poems*, 2003.

p. 103. 'Half-hearted', Brendan Kennelly, Preface to *The Book of Judas: A Poem*, Northumberland: Bloodaxe Books, 1991.

p. 105. 'The Story of the Pencil', Paulo Coelho, *Like the Flowing River: Thoughts and Reflections*, London: HarperCollins, 2007. *Ser como o rio que flui* © 2006, Paulo Coelho.

p. 117. 'The Easter Challenge', Joyce Rupp. Used with permission of the publishers, Ave Maria Press, Inc., PO Box 428, Notre Dame, Indiana 46556, www.avemariapress.com.

p. 121. 'The Merton Prayer', Thomas Merton, *Thoughts in Solitude* (1958), New York: Farrar, Straus and Giroux, 1998.

p. 131. 'Take, Bless, Break and Give', Michael Drumm and Tom Gunning, *A Sacramental People Volume I: Initiation*, Dublin: Columba Press, 1999. Used with kind permission.

p. 137. 'The Difference', Grace L. Naessens. Reprinted by kind permission of the author.

p. 159. 'Christmas Prologue', *Cloth for the Cradle: Worship Resources and Readings for Advent, Christmas and Epiphany*, Glasgow: Wild Goose Publications, 1997. Words John L. Bello. Copyright © 1997 WGRG, Iona Community, Glasgow G2 3DH, Scotland. www.wgrg.co.uk.

p. 160. 'Christmas Lasts Forever', *Karl Rahner The Great Church Year: The Best of Karl Rahner's Homilies, Sermons, and Meditations*, New York: Crossroad, 1993.